Association for Middle Level Education

Middle School:

A Place to Belong & Become

Laurie Barron, Ed.D.
Patti Kinney

Printed in the United States of America.

ISBN 978-1-56090-293-5

William D. Waidelich, EdD, CAE—Executive Director
April Tibbles—Chief Communications Officer
Dawn Williams—Publicatons Manager/Designer
Marcia Meade-Hurst— Senior Member Center Specialist

Library of Congress Control Number: 2017955616

Association for Middle Level Education
4151 Executive Parkway, Suite 300
Westerville, Ohio 43081 | amle.org

Table of Contents

Acknowledgments

Woodrow Wilson once said, "We should not only use the brains we have but all that we can borrow," and we definitely took his advice in writing this book. Far too many people to list were involved in helping us frame, reframe, write, rewrite, organize, and reorganize this manuscript, but we especially want to acknowledge the tremendous help given to us by the following individuals:

This book would not have been completed without the amazing work of our editor, **Marj Frank.** She guided, encouraged, and challenged us from beginning to end and then took what we wrote, made it so much better, and helped us sound so much smarter! Our most sincere thanks and appreciation goes to her.

While we greatly appreciate **Rick Wormeli** for his willingness to write our foreword, we are even more grateful for his encouragement, comments, probing questions, and constructive feedback that helped us refine our thoughts and focus even more on the importance of *belonging* and *becoming*.

A big thanks also goes to **Judith Brough** for giving us valuable feedback on our first (very) rough draft. Her questions, comments, and edits were instrumental as we continued to revise and improve upon our initial manuscript.

Our work over the years with the students, staff, and parents at **Talent Middle School** in Oregon (Patti) and **Smokey Road Middle School** in Georgia and the **Evergreen School District** in Montana (Laurie) provided us with the knowledge, background, experience, and understanding of just how important the concepts of *belonging* and *becoming* are when it comes to providing the best education possible for young adolescents.

A book simply cannot be written without the support of **family and friends**. Thank you all for understanding and putting up with the numerous hours spent writing that pulled us away from spending time with each of you.

And finally, it would be heresy to write about the importance of student voice and not incorporate it in this book! A big thank you goes to the large number of **middle school students in the Flathead Valley of Montana** who served as our sounding boards and resident experts whenever we needed a student perspective. And while we can't name them all, we do want to give a shout out to Laurie's young adolescent daughter, **Emma Barron,** for her continued support and contributions.

Foreword by Rick Wormeli

Twenty years ago, differentiation expert, Carol Ann Tomlinson, made a comment in a keynote address that teaching in a diverse classroom was like the taming of the fox in Antoine de Saint-Exupery's, *The Little Prince*. This idea stuck with me in subsequent re-readings of the book, and I began to see the whole story as one about *belonging* and why it matters so much to humanity. In chapter 21 of *The Little Prince*, the little prince is curious about a wild fox that wishes to be tamed by the prince:

> "No," said the little prince. "I am looking for friends. What does that mean—'tame'?"
>
> "It is an act too often neglected," said the fox. "It means to establish ties."
>
> " 'To establish ties'?"
>
> "Just that," said the fox. "To me, you are still nothing more than a little boy who is just like a hundred thousand other little boys. And I have no need of you. And you, on your part, have no need of me. To you, I am nothing more than a fox like a hundred thousand other foxes. But if you tame me, then we shall need each other. To me, you will be unique in all the world. To you, I shall be unique in all the world …"

And later in the same chapter, the fox says,

> "My life is very monotonous...I hunt chickens; men hunt me. All the chickens are just alike, and all the men are just alike. And, in consequence, I am a little bored. But if you tame me, it will be as if the sun came to shine on my life. I shall know the sound of a step that will be different from all the others. Other steps send me hurrying back underneath the ground. Yours will call me, like music, out of my burrow. And then look: you see the grain-fields down yonder? I do not eat bread. Wheat is of no use to me. The wheat fields have nothing to say to me. And that is sad. But you have hair that is the color of gold. Think how wonderful that will be when you have tamed me! The grain, which is also golden, will bring me

back the thought of you. And I shall love to listen to the wind in the wheat …"

The fox gazed at the little prince, for a long time. "Please—tame me!" he said.

"I want to, very much," the little prince replied. "But I have not much time. I have friends to discover, and a great many things to understand."

"One only understands the things that one tames," said the fox. "Men have no more time to understand anything. They buy things all ready made at the shops. But there is no shop anywhere where one can buy friendship, and so men have no friends any more. If you want a friend, tame me …"

"What must I do, to tame you?" asked the little prince.

"You must be very patient," replied the fox.

—Excerpted from *The Little Prince*
by Antoine de Saint-Exupery, 1943, chapter 21

Adults have a true salve for stormy times of change: If we are patient and "establish ties" with others, we can be ourselves, rough edges and all, can weather any change, for we are more than accepted, we are valued. In such relationships, we can be kites in windswept skies, but our dangerous pull and dance will be no match for such strong tethers.

In his beautiful book, *The Hidden Life of Trees* (Greystone Books, 2015), Peter Wohlleben demonstrates the same parallels with trees: In times of stress, he says, trees not only depend on the entwined nature of their roots to fortify them against the wind, but they also share with one another the nutrients and water for photosynthesis, ensuring that those without access to either thrive. Living in relationship, each with a role to play in the nurture of one another, is *belonging*.

If we don't have ties or *belong* to someone else, on the other hand, we are perpetually in survival mode, rarely extending ourselves for fear of having nothing left to survive the day. We are on guard, too, against our realness, for others knowing who we are makes us vulnerable to them. In an already fragile world, we can't have that. Yet, at our most vulnerable times, we hope that we are known and valued by another. And just as with the collaborative trees, if we don't *belong*, we don't flourish— we don't *become*.

And so it is with young adolescents every day, only more so.

When it comes to "*becoming*," particularly in student-centered classrooms, no one can deny the influence of psychologist, Carl Rogers, particularly from his work in the 50s, 60s, and 70s. Rogers' insights were the touchstone for many of the practices we find successful today: collaborating with students in their learning, teachers as facilitators instead of merely lecturers, differentiation, and students feeling safe and empowered to solve their own problems.

In his helpful book, *50 Psychology Classics: Who We Are, How We Think, What We Do: Insight and Inspiration from 50 Key Books* (Nicholas Brealey, 2007) Tom Butler-Bowdon discusses Rogers' classic, *On Becoming a Person* (1961). Consider the potent connections to the modern educator's role in student development in these excerpts:

> In his training as a psychologist, Rogers [thought] that it was his job to analyze and treat the patient as if he or she was an object. But he came to the conclusion that it was more effective to actually let the patient, or client, guide the direction of the process...Rather than trying to 'fix' the client, Rogers felt it much more important to listen absolutely to what a person was saying...He asserted the right of the therapist to have a personality, to express emotions themselves...If he did not have an answer, he would not pretend he did...

> In short, [he] held that change would only happen through the experience of a relationship, and that it was the therapist's role to provide an environment in which personal growth might occur. ... The fulfilled person, he believed, should come to accept themselves "as a stream of *becoming*, not a finished product.

Rogers observed that people…were desperate to *become* their real selves, to be allowed to drop the false roles or masks with which they had approached life to date. They were usually very concerned with what others thought of them and what they ought to be doing in given situations. [and that] …They cease to be a rigid set of rules about who they must be, and are transformed into a person who can ask…the question "What does this mean to me?" They *become* a person, not just a reflection of society.

—Retrieved from http://www.butler-bowdon.com/carl-rogers---on-becoming-a-person.html, July 19, 2017

Wait – Individuals as, "a stream of *becoming*, not a finished product?" Moving from deficit thinking ("trying to fix the client") to listening to the student and facilitating personal growth? Dropping masks and *becoming* who we really are, not just reflections of perceived societal expectations? There is nothing here that isn't tied directly to working with students, ages 10 to 15. Laurie Barron and Patti Kinney are on to something when they offer the dual themes of *belonging* and *becoming*. There are not two better concepts that capture the middle school experience as well as these do.

Barron and Kinney's insights are timely. Today's political, religious, sexual orientation, race, and economic rhetoric and realities are growing more divisive, and xenophobia (fear of the other) is normalizing in unhealthy ways. Students and many of their teachers are relying more and more on external validations for mental/emotional balance, too, succumbing to moderate paranoia or anger if no one responds to a social media post within minutes of its posting: "What's wrong with me?" "Am I not worth at least a, 'like'?" "Did I do something wrong?" "Do I not matter?" Feelings of abandonment, threat to life, anger, loneliness, and violence exacerbate when we don't *belong*, lack identity, and fail to launch personally. We need these skilled mentors authoring this exceptional book.

Barron and Kinney are award-winning principals who've made major contributions to both their local communities and to the nation as a whole, let alone to the profession around the world, but they have the souls of classroom teachers, and boy, does that practicality come through. There are dozens of classroom examples and insights here, and seriously deep, "seasoned veteran" understanding of the unique nature of young adolescents and how to work with them. Refreshingly, their ideas are actionable, and they are sensitive to budget constraints, providing work-arounds when finances are an issue. They've been there, done that, and bought the souvenir t-shirt. Now, they're candid, going all, "Trip Advisor Review," on us, describing what's what. Man, I'm glad to be in the room when they do; their combined experience is stunning.

Laurie and Patti are up to speed on the latest thinking in multiple areas, including executive function, self-efficacy, differentiation, special education, staff development, reflective practices, and more. All the helpful, go-to thinkers and doers of our profession are here, too: Kohlberg, George, Swaim, Deci, Ryan, Lounsbury, Rosenthal, Jacobson, Boaler, Comer, Brooks, Berckemeyer, Crocker, Dewey, Dweck, Guskey, Kohn, Compton, Curwin, Eichhorn, and even, Winnie-the-Pooh, among others.

Several elements readers will appreciate include Laurie and Patti looking at all of this through the principals' eyes, organizing and structuring schools and programs so as to cultivate the school's deeply held values. We also get clear advice on how to sustain the middle school concept and all its pieces even in times of political change, and specific things we can do daily to promote these elements, not just in big, rah-rah events.

I'm struck, too, by how many of their insights in working with students transfer to leaders' work with teachers. The sections on characteristics of young adolescents and, "Putting It Into Practice," collectively would make a cogent focus for an entire course on middle level education, suitable for specialized certification programs. In addition, we can incorporate many of these strategies as we conduct ourselves with one another and as we aspire to improve our own practices. An easy "a-ha" inspired by the book is to look at ourselves: How do we teachers and administrators learn to *belong* and actively help others *belong*? How do we *become*? And how can taking such similar journeys as our students make us better educators for them?

Let's actively pursue these ideas, not just post them on the teacher's lounge wall and let them fade into the ceaseless dyne and drone of competing education reforms. This is the raw DNA of middle level success for our students, ready to combine base pairs and form nucleotides – the stuff of life, sparked by inspired readers who yell, "Heck-yeah, I'm in!" The book is that kind of oxygen.

When we die, what will be our lasting testimony? I imagine it will be commentary on how we lived and how we made others feel: Were we kind? Did we contribute to the world? Did we forgive others? In what did we believe so strongly that we were fearless? Did we conduct ourselves in such a way as to merit others' connections to us? Did we follow our dream of what could be? Did we let ourselves be thwarted? Did we ever *become*? Did we tame a wild fox or three?

Let's establish ties and embrace the many streams of *becoming* gathered in our classrooms. Let's make sure each chrysalis is fully nourished and left undisturbed. What an honor it is to be given such responsibility, and what a relief it is to be given the tools to do it properly! Not all are called to such work, but Laurie and Patti *belong* to us and we to them. With their words here, we *become* what our students need us to be.

Rick Wormeli
Teacher, Teacher Trainer
Columnist for *AMLE Magazine*
Author of *Meet Me in the Middle*
October 2017

Preface

Two words sparked the creation of this book—words that kept popping up in all our discussions of middle level students—words so powerful that, before long, we knew they had to be not only the key ideas of a book but the title as well! As we reflected on students we have had opportunities to know and teach, the schools we have led and observed, the teachers we have mentored and enjoyed as colleagues, the programs we have examined and developed—in a sort of "aha" moment, we were struck by how often *belonging* and *becoming* were centerpieces of the conversation. This reminded us of learning the handy skill of reducing fractions to a common denominator. When we learn to do this, all of a sudden our eyes open to the value of the numbers; we see them in the same terms, can compare them, work with them, and gain a clearer understanding of equivalencies. We've found a common denominator in our work—a thread that ties together concerns of students, effective middle level practices, and young adolescent development. **That common factor is the profound need and desire for young adolescents to find places where they feel they can** *belong* **and can discover who they are and who they want to** *become.*

The more we looked at the words *belong* and *become* (and the broad meanings behind them), the more we realized just how foundational are these concepts to the development of young adolescents and thus to the goals, passions, and purposes of our work with young adolescents. This brought us to the questions, "Why are *belonging* and *becoming* critical to the education of our students?" and "What can middle level schools and educators do to help students *belong* and *become*?" And thus this book was born—to explore and share some answers for those questions.

Not long ago, I (Patti) ran across a copy of a speech that four eighth graders (representing a variety of cultural backgrounds) gave to their peers, parents, teachers, and other audience members during the eighth grade recognition assembly at the middle school where I was principal. Laurie and I were both amazed at how well their words, written years ago, capture the essence of what we would like to share with other middle level educators about *belonging* and *becoming.*

My name is America. This is Calvin, Paty, and Alexia. Lucia also helped with the writing of this speech.

Calvin: When I was first asked to do this speech, I wanted to know a bit of my family's history, so I talked to my mom and asked her what continent we originated from. It turned out we've been here for generations. But there are other families here who are fairly new to this country—many immigrants seeking a better way of life. Many of them have become my close friends over these three years at TMS.

America: My mother emigrated from Mexico 16 years ago. I, however, was born and raised here in Oregon. We went back to Mexico when I was four years old for almost two years, where I had the opportunity to meet my grandparents for the first time.

Paty: My dad emigrated from Mexico 25 years ago, leaving a family behind to find a better life. My mother waited five years before joining my father. She left an infant son in the care of my grandmother. It would be five years before they were reunited.

Alexia: In modern American culture, lots of times different backgrounds are lost. My mother emigrated from South Korea to the United States in the 1980s and was only able to visit her homeland once more before her death. Being Asian American is important to me; I can live in modern day culture but must always remember my ethnic background.

Ours are only a few of many stories behind each unique student here at TMS. In school, we have found a home and have been both accepted and scorned for our cultural backgrounds. Our three years have combined to one giant learning experience—an awakening to the vast world that lies ahead. From the moment we set foot on Bulldog territory, we gained a new sense of freedom. Over these past three years, we students have made rules and set standards that go beyond the classroom and the parent handbook. We have strived to earn respect and identity, and through this, our consciousness has been raised to yet another level. Many students begin to find themselves in middle school. However, we also come to have a better understanding of those around us.

While important life lessons are learned from rules like "turn in your work on time", "listen when the teacher is talking", "always come to class prepared", *and* "don't run in the halls", *middle school teaches even deeper, more personal lessons. We've come to learn when to hold our tongues and when to speak out, how to treat our friends and those whom we are not so fond of so that we can make it through the day, and how to show the people who we care about that we truly appreciate their friendship. We've learned what does and does not make somebody smile, the best things to say when confronted by a bully—if we need say anything at all—and that in the end, the easiest person to be is oneself. Without every up and every down we have had at this school, surely none of us would be the people we have become.*

To our teachers: we would like to thank each and every one of you who has ever scolded, encouraged, or congratulated us. And as for the students: thank YOU for making school one hundred times more exciting than textbooks, worksheets, and dull pencils. Whether our families are new to this country, or have been here for generations, Talent Middle School has housed us all. Thank you, TMS, for three years of growth—both academic and otherwise— and for memories that will stay with us much longer than the faded pages of a 2008 yearbook.

Creating a middle level school where students can *belong* and, as well, where they *become* what they are capable of being personally and academically is a difficult, complex task. We freely admit that we don't have all the answers. But our nearly 60 combined years of experience working with young adolescents enable us to share stories and practices that are built upon both foundations of effective middle level education and the development, needs, and possibilities of young adolescents. Our desire is for this book to give readers practical information and strategies to help them establish and nurture an environment where the young adolescents entrusted to them can both *belong* and *become*. We wish you well on this journey.

— *Laurie and Patti*

PART I
Foundations for Belonging and Becoming

If you have ever bought a house, had a house built, or even watched a home renovation show on TV, you know the critical importance of the building's foundation. Without a solid base, the building will not support the rest of the structure; it will sink, throwing other things out of alignment as you build upward. Places built without foundations or with shaky foundations will eventually crumble and fall down. So it is with schools.

In the absence of a firm foundation—changes made, ideas implemented, and strategies used are likely to be temporary. They'll have minimal impact on the school's overall culture. Part I of this book lays the foundation needed for a school that promotes *belonging* and *becoming*. This includes the following elements for a lasting base. Each is critical, but none stands alone; they are interdependent and only work well when implemented together.

1) A common understanding of what *belonging* and *becoming* mean for your school.

2) School policies and practices solidly based on the developmental characteristics, needs, and experiences of young adolescents.

3) An organizational (school) structure that promotes respectful, inclusive relationships and that provides opportunities and support for students' personal development and academic accomplishments.

Putting it into practice: At the end of each chapter in this book, you'll find a page that offers concrete strategies for engaging with the ideas of the chapter. Use these to spark discussions, gather feedback, evaluate current practices, expand your skills with a process, set goals, and decide on action steps. Adapt the ideas as needed for individual self-reflection or for working in pairs with a colleague, as a team or small group, or as an entire staff.

Chapter 1

Build a Common Understanding of Belonging and Becoming

Belong | verb | be·long | bi-ˋlȯŋ, bē-ˈlȯŋ |: to be a part of; to be connected with

Become | verb | be·come | bi-ˈkəm, bē-ˈkəm |: to come or grow to be, develop into

---

Early adolescence has often been referred to as the "wonder years"—an appropriate label, as the development in this span of years gives the kids themselves (and the adults who live and work with them) much to **wonder** about! In this period of time, these youngsters experience some of the most profound physical, cognitive, social, and emotional changes in their lives—the most growth since birth to age three. But what's significantly different from previous growth spurts is that, at this stage, they are able to recognize the changes.

And with that recognition comes such concerns, fears, and questions as: "Am I normal?" "Why is my best friend more physically developed than I am?" "Why am I happy one moment and sad the next?" "Do I fit in?" "How do I fit in?" "Am I really accepted by my friends?" "Why do adults keep asking me what I want to be when I grow up when I haven't a clue?" "Why can't I understand what the math teacher is trying to explain?" "Why does my best friend from elementary school no longer talk to me?" "I hate this new haircut; everyone's going to stare at me tomorrow." "How can I grow toward independence from adults yet remain connected to them?" "I'm too fat, too skinny, too tall, too short . . ." And the list goes on and on and on.

Far too often, we adults get caught up in the busyness of schooling—covering the curriculum, collecting homework, filling out paperwork, meeting state standards, administering state tests, etc. In doing so, we often forget to take time to listen to and address authentic student concerns. If we do stop to examine their worries, we find that at the heart of the apprehensions is a compelling need to *belong*, to be accepted, and to discover who they are and what they are capable of doing and *becoming*. As middle level educators, we simply are not doing our jobs if we fail to help our students address these needs in safe, positive environments. We have been entrusted with the care, nurturing, and education of young adolescents. To do that, we must work to give our students a sense of *belonging*. In addition, we must offer many tools and supports to help them discover (and move toward) the many things they are capable of *becoming*. To begin to accomplish these goals, we must agree on a shared understanding of what is meant, in our own schools, by *belonging* and *becoming*.

Belonging

All human beings want to *belong*; we each have a deep-seated need to feel connected to others and to be a valued and accepted member of a group—whether it be family, friends, a class, or a school. And young adolescents are at a time in their lives when this need is particularly strong. They desperately want to *belong* and figure out how they can fit in.

In her landmark study of students' sense of *belonging* in schools, Carol Goodenow (1993) defined *belonging* as students' sense of "psychological membership in the school or classroom, that is, the extent to which students feel personally accepted, respected, included, and supported by others in the school environment" (p. 80).

Heather P. Libbey (2007), who studies students' relationships to their schools, describes school *belonging* to be a situation in which students "feel close to, a part of, and happy at school; feel that teachers care about the students and treat them fairly; get along with teachers and other students, and feel safe at school" (p. 52).

Students who *belong*

- Feel a sense of identification with a group.
- Feel safe at school—both physically and psychologically.
- Feel that they have a voice in school.
- Feel respected.
- Believe in their own indispensability to the group.
- Trust their teachers and their peers.
- Believe that they have as much value as anyone else.
- Are confident that others see them as valuable.
- Feel securely connected with others in their school and classes.
- See themselves as being part of a supportive community.
- Not only feel support but also are able to accept it.
- Feel wanted and needed.
- Feel like individuals, not stereotypes.
- Perceive and trust that the belongingness they feel is likely to continue.

Students who experience school as a place where they *belong* might say:

There is mutual respect here.

Everybody matters.

This school is committed to every student.

I feel that I belong to my class (team, school).

People are not left out.

I feel trust, and I feel trusted.

I have something to contribute.

I do not feel threatened.

We don't put each other down here.

Students here are connected.

I feel comfortable interacting in my classroom.

Everyone is involved in helping everyone belong.

There are no kids here who don't have friends.

We have each other's backs.

Why Does *Belonging* Matter?

A wide body of research supports a multiplicity of positive benefits that accompany a student's feeling of connection to his or her school and the adults and peers in it. In several meta-analyses of research on school *belonging* and school connection (including focus on secondary school settings), it has been found that *belonging* is **positively associated** with psychological, social, and academic functioning in school across a range of variables. These include self-esteem, self-efficacy, optimism, social competence, trust of

> **Belonging is positively associated with psychological, social, and academic functioning in school across a range of variables.**

others, building relationships, cognitive performance, academic work, attitudes toward learning, expectancy of success, intrinsic motivation, participation, effort, classroom engagement, autonomy, physical health, academic self-efficacy, and general life satisfaction. In addition, students with a strong sense of *belonging* take greater advantage of learning opportunities and do better in school. Compared to students who have little sense of *belonging*, they are more fully and enthusiastically engaged in learning, are more likely to see classes as interesting and useful, are more likely to persevere, are more open to critical feedback, and have improved ability to respond in healthy ways to situations of adversity. They have less disruptive behavior, fewer negative emotions in class, lower stress, fewer behavior problems, and lower absenteeism (Anderman, L., 1999, 2003; Allen & Bowles, 2012; Furrer and Skinner, 2003; O'Brien & Bowles, 2013; Romero, 2015; Wingspread, 2004).

Many students do not enjoy a sense of *belonging* at school. This can leave them feeling out of place, alienated, or rejected. The failure to feel a sense of *belonging* is negatively associated with emotional distress, loneliness, increased anxiety, boredom, and depression—and with frustration and sadness in situations of academic engagement. Disconnected students experience increased self-consciousness, social isolation, and deteriorating motivation. They are more likely to exhibit disruptive behavior and violence at school than students who feel they *belong* (Baumeister & Leary, 1995; Furrer & Skinner, 2003; Wingspread, 2004). Sadly, a common thread among much of the violence that has occurred in schools is that the perpetrators were isolated, not included in social groups, and often felt harassed or bullied.

In addition to missing the benefits of *belonging* described in the lists and paragraphs above, students who don't feel they *belong* are at risk for a variety of academic, social, or behavioral problems. When examining the connection between school relatedness and academic engagement, Furrer and Skinner (2003) explained that "children who feel unimportant or rejected by key partners are more likely to become frustrated, bored, or alienated from learning activities, which in turn interferes with their academic progress; poor performance coupled with disaffection erodes social support, leading children to feel further estranged" (p. 158). These findings give us more reasons why *belonging* matters.

Not all students are solidly on one or the other end of the *belonging* spectrum. There are some who might say they are confident they *belong*. There are others who are seriously disengaged—feeling like complete outsiders. But there are many (perhaps the majority) who are in the middle and fit the following description: "When students are uncertain about whether they *belong*, they are vigilant for cues in the environment that signal whether or not they *belong*, fit in, or are welcome there. This hyper vigilance and extra stress uses up cognitive resources that are essential for learning, diminishing their performance and discouraging them from building valuable relationships" (Romero, 2015, p. 2).

In 2003, the Johnson Foundation funded a conference at the Wingspread Conference Center in Wisconsin, sponsored by the U.S. Centers for Disease Control and Prevention's Division of Adolescent and School Health. A group of key researchers and representatives from the education and health sectors focused on the state of school connectedness and its effects on health and education outcomes for students. After a detailed review of research and in-depth discussions, the group issued the *Wingspread Declaration on School Connections* (2004). This set of insights and strategies, they stated, "should form the basis for creating school and classroom environments where all students, independent of academic capacity, are engaged and feel a part of the educational endeavor" (p. 233).

The *Wingspread Declaration* and all the implications of the research on *belonging* show that schools need greater awareness of the relationship between *belonging* and both academic success and psychological and physical health. And beyond the awareness, schools must actively work to develop and support student well-being. All students deserve the security of authentic *belonging*—the assurance that they are valued and genuinely have a place in the school community, not for what they can do but rather just for who they are.

Becoming

Just think of all the things we want our middle level students to be and *become*—all the qualities we hope they'll develop; the academic content, skills, and processes we think they need to master; the personal and interpersonal behaviors we believe are healthy for them to acquire; and the understandings we're convinced they need to internalize! *Becoming* is a complex concept—a lifelong process with, oh, so many facets and meanings.

A major part of *becoming* is navigating through the journey of growing up, of maturing, of *becoming* an adult. But that doesn't happen overnight or in one fell swoop; it's a process with many components, variations, and bumps along the way. Most importantly, it is unique to each individual. When asked what it means to grow up, many middle level students think of it as living on their own, going away to college, starting their first real job, finding a career, and being financially independent. But *becoming* is not all about what happens for students in their futures. They are *becoming* every day; one way or another, they are developing, learning, growing, gaining autonomy, taking more charge of their own lives, and changing. We must help them right now to develop such critical components of maturity as making good decisions, taking responsibility for their actions and their commitments, accepting the consequences of their choices and actions, and understanding that what they say and do can affect others.

Of course, part of *becoming* for our students is learning academic skills, honing various processes for continued learning, and building a necessary base of knowledge. Yes, we know that students need to be critical thinkers and learn to find, process, evaluate, and use information. We want them to take on challenges and strive for mastery. We want them to *become* active listeners, competent writers, proficient readers, and capable mathematicians. We want them to be articulate and able to express themselves clearly and to engage in discussions productively. We want them to be able to reflect on actions and ideas—to think about and process their own thoughts and behaviors. And we certainly want them to be able to make reasoned evaluations about messages from media, pop culture, and peers that bombard them constantly— and to filter out what is untrue, irrelevant, harmful, or inappropriate.

However, it is not only the task of middle level schools to promote academic skills and successes. It is also schools' mission to provide students with opportunities to explore, to make choices, to take risks, to grow in autonomy, to learn to interact with others, to be curious and inventive, to try new endeavors, to be able to recover from failure, to be exposed to the world beyond their community, to dream big, to set goals, and to discover what their futures may hold.

If we are to prepare our students to participate productively in a democratic society (and in all the groups of which they are a part within their society), we must think far beyond content knowledge. We wish for our students to be and *become* young adolescents, older adolescents, and adults who are caring and compassionate—with hopeful, optimistic attitudes toward learning and life. We wish to see them *become* seasoned problem solvers and independent, lifelong learners.

We want our students to understand how to develop and maintain positive relationships, cope with peer pressure, demonstrate tolerance and acceptance of others, and develop the people skills needed to learn, work, and interact with others. They need to recognize the developmental changes that are happening within them and know how these changes can impact their emotions and actions. They must learn to handle anger, cope with disappointment, channel emotions in positive ways, and both understand and deal with the stresses that the roller-coaster ride of early adolescence can bring. We want them to develop resilience and perseverance. Yes, we want so much for our students! And, yes, it is an overwhelming task.

Middle level students often come to us with hopes and dreams for what their futures hold. Some of their dreams are realistic, while others could be called "fairy-tale" thinking (if you want it and wait long enough, then magically, it will come true, all will be well, and you will live happily ever after).

When I (Patti) taught sixth grade, I kicked off a unit of study on life-cycles with an activity where students created their own life timelines. They were to choose important events that had already happened in their lives and then predict events in their futures. Students illustrated their timelines on long strips of adding machine tape and displayed them on a bulletin board. I remember a conversation with a student who was examining the predicted lives of his classmates. I had noticed a common thread among most of the boys' lifelines (his included)—they were going to be NBA or NFL stars—and asked him if he thought that was a reasonable prediction. I'll never forget his response: "Mrs. Kinney, we know it's not likely to happen, but just let us have our dreams!"

It's a fine line that educators have to walk. We don't want to belittle or impede their dreams, but we also need to help them discover just what they will need to do in order to realistically accomplish their dreams, to *become* what they dream of *becoming*. Fortunately, unrealistic dreams and ambitions usually change with maturity, so we need to help our students develop their skills and see the options and possibilities beyond that one possibly unrealistic dream. We owe it to our students to do the best we can to prepare them for adulthood, regardless of whether or not that sixth grade dream comes true.

Why Does *Becoming* Matter?

The list of what we hope for our students to *become* is long. You could add many skills, qualities, and behaviors beyond those mentioned here. It is important to realize that the *becoming* process is not something we do for our students. Certainly, families, schools, and others in society can nurture aspects of *becoming*, and many factors in students' lives (such as peers and pop culture) contribute to the process (positively or negatively). But inevitably, willingness to learn, effort, engagement, integration, and self-determination flow from the individual himself or herself.

It might seem strange to even ask the question "Why does *becoming* matter?" The answers seem so obvious. *Becoming*, after all, is what human life is about—and is the focus of all schooling (and parenting)! One look at the aspects of *becoming* that we've already described gives an answer (just notice how important all those qualities are)! We can encapsulate what is at the heart of *becoming* with the term *self-determination*—the ability to make choices and decisions and to set and achieve goals based on one's own intrinsic motivation and volition (and not dependent upon outside influence). All the facets of *becoming* we've described, and the many more we did not delineate, need the student to be a full participant. We educators must nurture that intrinsic motivation and volition to give each of our students the best chance at *becoming*.

> **Becoming, after all, is what human life is about—and is the focus of all schooling (and parenting)!**

According to self-determination theory, there are three innate psychological needs: autonomy, competence, and relatedness. When these needs are met, the individual moves toward self-motivation, self-regulation, constructive social development, and overall personal well-being (Deci & Ryan, 1985; Ryan & Deci, 2000b). Through extensive research into conditions that foster or impede self-determination, authors

Richard Ryan and Edward Deci found that it flourished in social contexts (such as school) that supported and encouraged these three needs. On the other hand, conditions that included "excessive control, nonoptimal challenges, and lack of connectedness," undermined the growth and expression of self-determination (2000, p. 76). (Notice that "relatedness" (aka *belonging*) is an integral part of this triad of basic needs!)

Ryan and Deci (2000) recognized the power of the social contexts in which growing humans are imbedded. They emphasized that the natural tendencies toward positive cognitive development, personal development, and well-being do not develop automatically; they need ongoing nurturing in social settings. The authors of the self-determination theory adamantly entreat all practitioners who work with growing human beings to integrate practices that address the three psychological needs in order to facilitate the development of these natural tendencies. Consider social contexts—think of how much of their lives children spend at school! As educators, then, we must become very knowledgeable about the conditions and practices that enhance (rather than undermine) *becoming* in positive ways.

Implementing the Belonging-Becoming Partnership

Becoming is closely entwined with *belonging*. Young adolescents need a place to *belong* so that they are free to *become*—to develop skills, knowledge, and character, determine strengths, discern potential, and discover passions. Paired together, *belonging* and *becoming* can be described as a powerful interdependent relationship. When students feel that they *belong* to a school community, their chances for deeper personal and academic growth (*becoming*) escalate; when students are more academically and personally successful (aspects of *becoming*), their senses of *belonging* increase.

Next to families, schools are the settings with the greatest potential to help children in these two foundational processes. When we, the authors, look at this powerful combination of needs in the lives of our students (the needs to *belong* and *become*), we

1) Are adamant that schools be aware of them and the dynamic interaction between them.
2) Feel the urgency of schools making it a priority to address these needs.
3) Are invigorated by the possibilities of what can happen for middle level students when we take deliberate actions to address them together.

In this book, we share practices and understandings for helping students in their quests to *belong* and *become*—for at the heart of things, that's what everything we do at the middle level is about! In her book, *Our Last Best Shot: Guiding our Children Through Early Adolescence* (2001), Laura Sessions Stepp argues that the middle level school years offer us what is truly "our last best shot" at making a difference in the future success of students. This is because most of them are still young and resilient enough to allow us to help them travel through the maze of early adolescence and find the path that leads to healthy, responsible present and future lives.

Effective middle level educators understand this urgency, recognizing that young adolescents need an environment focused on their unique requirements. They also recognize that these students deserve to be with adults who understand and appreciate them, and who will work to meet their needs both in and out of the classroom.

Creating a place where students can *belong* and *become* is a challenging proposition with no easy answers or silver bullet strategies. Middle level students are often more interested in *belonging* to a friendship group than to their school. They tend to be more concerned about impressing their friends than their teachers. They may be more worried about wearing the right brand of clothing than turning in their home-work. They may be more focused on *becoming* players in the NBA or the USWNT (women's soccer) than *becoming* accomplished students.

Plans and actions to help young adolescents *belong* and *become* must be infused into all of the policies, practices, programs, and relationships in a school and in its classrooms. We know that schools are struggling with budget issues, staffing cuts, the public's and lawmakers' overemphasis on academic achievement and passing the "test," and sometimes with a general misunderstanding from outsiders of what middle level education needs to be. Those issues and others may be reasons why the task seems insurmountable at times. But they can't be used as excuses for not trying. And, thankfully, many effective ideas for addressing *belonging* and *becoming* can be incorporated into school and classroom practices without additional costs or staffing. We urge you to make your lists of components, qualities, and skills related to *belonging* and *becoming* (as recommended at the end of this chapter) and keep them posted—visible at all times.

In their book *The Life-giving Home*, authors Sally and Sarah Clarkson (2016) described how to create a home that is foundational to life. We think their introductory words apply equally to creating a life-giving school:

> All people need a place where their roots can grow deep and they always feel like they belong and have a loving refuge.
> And all people need a place that gives wings to their dreams, nurturing possibilities of who they might become (p. 6).

Putting It into Practice

As an individual, team, small group, or entire staff, use some of these activities to spark discussions, reflect on your current practices or situations, listen to others, or set goals.

1. Use a 1, 2, 4, 8 process to define what *belonging* and *becoming* mean at your school. Ask each person to write down her own definition of *belonging*; then pair up with a colleague to combine definitions into one agreeable to both; then combine pairs into groups of four and repeat; and once more have groups of four combine to groups of eight. Have each group share its definition and look for commonalities among the groups. Repeat the process using the word *becoming*. Even if you and other staff members in your school or district are already committed to enhancing *belonging* and *becoming*, it will be a valuable exercise to find commonality in your understanding of the concepts. In addition, this will set the stage for sharing successful practices, broadening your efforts, and brainstorming how school staff can coordinate efforts in the best interest of the students.

2. Divide the staff into six groups and set up six stations around the room for a gallery walk. Stations 1-3 should each have butcher paper or sticky-back paper with one of the following questions. For stations 4-6, use the same questions with *becoming* substituted for *belonging*.

    —   If students felt they belonged at this school, what might we hear them say?

    —   If students felt they belonged at this school, what would teachers do and say?

    —   If students felt they belonged at this school, what outcomes would we experience?

Place one group in front of each station and ask members to write down what they see as answers to the questions. After a set amount of time, rotate groups. The next group reads what has been written, stars important ideas, puts question marks by ideas that need clarification, and adds its own ideas to the list. Rotate through until each group arrives back at its first station. Have each small group read through the answers and choose a few items to share with the entire group. Lists from each station can later be typed up and used for further discussion.

3. Hold focus groups with students to discover their thoughts and experiences on *belonging* and *becoming*. Ask them: "What does it mean to *belong*? To *become*?" "What's happening at school that makes you feel as if you *belong*? That you can *become*?" "What improvements are needed at this school to help students *belong* or *become*?" As a part of such exploration, you might use student-ready surveys such as those shown in Appendix F on pages 242–243. Be sure the groups are heterogeneously mixed across grade levels, genders, abilities, social groups, ethnicities, etc.

Chapter 2

Understand Young Adolescents

"At no other time in the life cycle are the chances of finding one's self and losing one's self so closely aligned."

- Erik Erickson

When educators set out to create settings where *belonging* and *becoming* can flourish for middle level students, we must first understand just who the students are and where they are in the course of both processes. It has long been recognized that early adolescence is a developmental stage separate from both childhood and full adolescence and that the young adolescents themselves have a set of unique characteristics. And it's no secret that one of the prime markers of the stage is the wide variation for individuals in timing and manifestation of the characteristics! This means that we need to know our students both as a developmental group and as individuals. The stronger the understanding educators have about the cognitive, social, emotional, moral, psychological, and physical development of their students, the better are the chances of helping them grow academically and personally—in all the aspects related to *belonging* and *becoming*.

So, begin by picturing what it might be like to be a young adolescent (or by remembering what it was to be one—after all, every one of us was one). In his book *Managing the Madness: A Practical Guide to Understanding Young Adolescents and Classroom Management*, Jack Berckemeyer (2018) gives us this snapshot:

> As young adolescents go through changes highly powered by hormones, they experience such new habits and impulses as increased twitching, a constant need for movement, and rapid mood swings. They can go from having vast amounts of energy at their desks (or OUT of their desks) to sleeping on the floor—in a matter of minutes. You can assign a silent writing, reading, or research activity and then watch a young adolescent male make the most unique facial expressions while his arm is swinging around in the air. Seemingly unable to control his body movements, he lets out a gigantic, loud sigh that could cause a tsunami halfway across the world. If you summon the courage to ask, "Are you okay?" he'll look at you and say, "WHAT?" He is totally clueless that he has released an earth-shaking amount of energy in just a few seconds.
>
> Yes, they tap, click, pat, shuffle, hum, chatter, whisper, make animal noises, burp, pass gas, and make faces—usually all within the first two minutes of class. They giggle, gasp, hide under hair or hoodies, guffaw, hold their noses, and react to one another in all sorts of ways from goading to groaning to applauding (p. 45).

In our memories, it was those years between elementary and high school during which we most struggled to *belong* and to discover who we were and what we might *become*. And now, with a young adolescent daughter in the midst of middle school, I (Laurie) see that many of my daughter's peers (who physically appear to range in ages from 9 to 15 but who in reality are only 13) are struggling to "fit in" and to get clear senses of their abilities, talents, and goals.

In the early days of the middle school movement (the mid 1960s), Dr. Donald Eichhorn (1966) wrote the first book about creating middle level schools. In *The Middle School*, he presented an argument for a suitable educational environment to be designed around the specific developmental characteristics of this age group. He coined the word *transescents* to describe middle grades students—referring to the developmental stage beginning just before puberty and extending through early adolescence.

The *transescent* label never caught on, but Mary Compton, a former Association for Middle Level Education president and professor at the University of Georgia, used it as the title for the following poem. Just substitute *young adolescent* for *transescent*, and we think you'll find it as relevant today as it was then.

Who Are Transescents?

Girls who play with Barbie dolls and girls who could compete in the Miss Teenage America contest...

Boys who look like short playing cards turned sideways and boys who already look like grown men...

Girls who don't know where babies come from and those who are experimenting to find out "for sure"...

Boys who play with toy dump trucks and those who can operate real ones...

Youngsters who play with Tinker Toys and those who can dismantle, repair, and reassemble an automobile engine...

Those who believe their parents are the smartest people in the world and those who wonder how such stupid, old-fashioned people have survived so long...

Kids who can't read their own names and those whose noses seem to be always in a book...

Youngsters who rate the opposite sex somewhere between spinach and milk-of-magnesia and those who are "on the make"...

Those who munch chocolate bars and those who pop amphetamines...

Those who guzzle Cokes and those who will soon be incurable alcoholics...

Those who meet the world with easy smiles and contagious laughter and those who are already being propelled by unbearable pressures toward the taking of their own lives...

These are transescents (as quoted in Swaim & Kinney, 2009, pp. 19-20).

Embracing Young Adolescent Development

Effective middle level teachers have learned how to appreciate and make the most of their students' developmental characteristics rather than fight against them. For example, they understand well that young adolescents have strong needs to socialize. They know that young brains actually learn best in concert with other brains! So they don't expect students to sit quietly for long time periods without interaction. They know that one of the most effective ways to increase students' senses of *belonging* is to get them working together. They want students to cooperate and communicate; they know how many academic, social, and emotional needs this strengthens. So they build learning activities around this need to socialize. (Teachers also realize that thwarting this need is guaranteed to lead to classroom management issues!)

> **Effective middle level teachers have learned how to appreciate and make the most of their students' developmental characteristics rather than fight against them.**

Teachers need to make plans and choices about what can foster *belonging*. But we can't do this unless we know the specifics of behaviors, attitudes, and situations in which our students do and do not experience *belonging*. Only when we understand just where they are in the process of those many aspects of *becoming* (academically, cognitively, socially, and emotionally) can we catch clues as to what procedures to use, what skills to teach, and what opportunities to offer. As we deepen our awareness of various aspects of their development, we get better and better at seeing specific actions we can take in our classrooms to help our students *belong* and *become* in many ways.

The need to socialize is just one of many characteristics to incorporate into our learning plans. Here are some other examples of ways that the understanding of students' development can inform and direct choices for our schools and classrooms.

Physical Development

Because young adolescents . . .

- Are experiencing rapid, irregular physical growth.
- Are undergoing bodily changes that may cause poor motor coordination.
- Are developing sexually.
- Experience mood swings, abrupt transitions from alertness and high energy to fatigue and lethargy.
- Often make poor food choices.
- Need plenty of rest and sleep (and tend not to get enough).
- Need frequent and somewhat continuous movement.

Then educators must . . .

- Vary the pace of lessons and incorporate movement.
- Assure individuals they are not the "only one" experiencing difficulties.
- Develop a comprehensive health and physical education program relevant to students' specific needs and capabilities.
- Plan opportunities for all students to succeed at physical accomplishments.
- Encourage adequate sleep, nutrition, and hydration.
- Help students understand their personal talents, skills, proficiencies, and inadequacies.

Cognitive Development

Because young adolescents . . .

- Have a wide range of intellectual abilities.
- Are curious, especially about the things that interest them.
- Are more willing to learn material they consider useful and relevant.
- Are increasing in their ability to think abstractly and metacognitively.
- Tend to be egocentric and can have difficulty seeing another's viewpoint.

Then educators must . . .

- Build lessons from concrete to abstract.
- Ask questions that require higher levels of thinking: "What if . . . ?" "How do you know . . . ?" "What led you to that conclusion?" "Can you describe your thinking about this?" "How is this valuable to you?" "How does this make a difference?"
- Create an environment where taking cognitive risks is encouraged, supported, and safe.
- Involve them actively in the learning—have them show AND tell AND do.
- Give them time to think—to process, to let ideas "gel," to explore different ideas.
- Be prepared for off-the-wall responses.

Social Development

Because young adolescents . . .

- Are concerned with acceptance and seek approval from peers.
- Can be argumentative.
- Experience flashes of social consciousness.
- Are self-conscious in social settings.
- Often reject adult standards or viewpoints on social issues.
- Follow social trends and fads.
- Are highly influenced by social media and pop culture.
- Can demonstrate extremes of social shyness or extroversion.

Then educators must . . .

- Design appropriate school-based social activities.
- Promote and model acceptance by adults and peers.
- Help students understand how they fit into the complex roles society expects of them.
- Provide opportunities for students to work and interact with others from different social, economic, and academic groups and backgrounds.
- Plan situations in which they can identify and evaluate messages and influences from social media and pop culture.
- Include community involvement and service learning in the curriculum.

Emotional Development

Because young adolescents . . .

- Experience chemical and hormonal changes and imbalances.
- Often overreact to seemingly minor issues.
- May look like adults but emotionally resemble children.
- Are increasingly aware of themselves, individually and in comparison to others.
- Tend to be unrealistically self-critical.
- Are easily offended.
- Are basically hopeful.

Then educators must . . .

- Understand and accept the typical behaviors of the age group. (Is the person being "appropriately" inappropriate or defiant?)
- Be honest, available role models.
- Be attentive listeners.
- Avoid sarcasm (that is not always seen as humor).
- Use praise and reinforcement in appropriate ways.
- Create an environment of acceptance, both with peers and adults.

Understanding Executive Function

Due to the rapid growth and multiple changes, middle level students are "in process" in just about every facet of their development. One cognitive aspect is still very much "under construction." How often do you notice a student

- Finding it difficult to transition between lessons, classes, or tasks?
- Getting easily distracted from her own work by anything happening around her?
- Not knowing where to begin to tackle three homework assignments?
- Making unrealistic plans?
- Having a hard time breaking a project down into manageable pieces?
- Struggling to finish what he starts?
- Rarely resisting the impulse to trip someone walking by?
- Forgetting something she learned and practiced yesterday?
- Drawing a blank when asked to summarize what he just did?
- Not seeming to have learned anything from a repeated mistake?
- Leaving all homework tasks to do until the last minute?
- Blurting out inappropriate comments without thinking?
- Sitting down to do a project without having thought to gather supplies?

Each of these is an indication of the incomplete development of the prefrontal cortex portion of the brain (which normally does not complete development until early adulthood). This is the part that controls what is known as *executive function*—the set of complex mental control mechanisms and skills that enable us to

- Make and follow through on plans.
- Filter distractions.

- Juggle multiple tasks.
- Move from one cognitive focus to another.
- Set and work toward goals.
- Curb impulses.
- Consider consequences before making decisions.
- Regulate behavior.

We use (and need) executive function to manage ourselves so that we can successfully navigate through life. According to the Center on the Developing Child at Harvard University,

> Scientists refer to these capacities as executive function and self-regulation—a set of skills that relies on three types of brain function: working memory, mental flexibility, and self-control. Children aren't born with these skills—they are born with the potential to develop them. The full range of abilities continues to grow and mature through the teen years and into early adulthood (2014, p. 1).

Understanding executive function reminds us that, regardless of what they look like physically, we are working with students whose brains aren't yet fully developed, who are not fully capable of thinking and acting the way (well-adjusted) adults think and act, and who aren't always (thank goodness) deliberately trying to drive us crazy. In fact, we were once just like them. (And since executive function develops at different paces, it needs a certain quality of experiences and interactions to emerge, and can change due to aging of the brain or outside influences—some adults are still like these young adolescents at times!) Yes, many of the habits or behaviors that seem irresponsible, intentionally annoying, or just "out to lunch" are normal for young adolescents. The status of their mental skills is to be expected.

Even the students, themselves, don't understand why they do what they do.

Even the students, themselves, don't understand why they do what they do. If you ask them, "Why did you do that?" or "What were you thinking?" often they will be honestly confused, tell you they know it was a poor decision, and say they just aren't sure why they behaved the way they did. And while we can't let them use "lack of brain development" as an excuse for inappropriate behaviors, students need to know that their still-developing brains may explain why it's sometimes difficult to control their actions, even when they know better.

As we focus on helping young adolescents *belong* and *become*, we see how important it is to help our students develop the full range of executive function capacities. These are critical to every aspect of *becoming* and *belonging* that we've identified and will continue to explore in this book. "When children have had opportunities to develop executive function and self-regulation skills successfully, both individuals and society experience lifelong benefits" (Center on the Developing Child, 2014, p. 1). These benefits include successful school achievement, positive behaviors, good health, and increased potential for success at work (Center on the Developing Child, 2014).

Educators must move beyond understanding the importance of executive function and the fact that these are still developing for our students. We must plan and take informed, specific actions to provide experiences and relationships to teach and strengthen these skills. Many of the practices that we'll recommend in upcoming chapters will focus on various aspects of executive function. You'll find more suggestions about ways to facilitate executive function in an article titled "Looking at Executive Function" (Wormeli, 2013) and in the book *Smart but Scattered Teens: The "Executive Skills" Program for Helping Teens Reach Their Potential* (Guare, Dawson, & Guare, 2013).

Examining Individual Differences

Those who work with young adolescents are well aware of the contradictions that occur within the age group as a whole, but we don't always remember to take into account the differences that occur among individual students. It is often far too easy to think of them, relate to them, or teach to them as one group—"those middle schoolers." John Lounsbury (2000), one of the founders of the middle school movement, made this observation in his essay "Understanding and Appreciating the Wonder Years":

> The dramatic physical changes do not occur at the same time or at the same rate. The fact that girls mature a year and a half to two years ahead of boys is widely recognized, but the tremendous variation in the rate and timing of the developmental processes of both boys and girls is not so well known. Some boys have achieved puberty before some girls have started. And what one child accomplishes in growth in 18 months may take up to three or more years in another. **As a result, a seventh grade class is likely to include men, women, and children** [emphasis by author]. It is virtually impossible for young adolescents to keep their chronological age in conformity with their social age, physical age, intellectual age, and/or social/sexual age (p. 1).

As examples of Dr. Lounsbury's observation, let's use two students who were classmates when I (Patti) taught sixth grade:

Kevin was about 5'6" when he started sixth grade. He was a sensitive student, concerned about how he fit in with the rest of the class. He struggled quite a bit in math, primarily because he had not yet begun to make the cognitive leap from concrete to abstract. By the end of the school year, he was nearly 6 feet tall, broad-shouldered, and deep-voiced. But he was still sensitive, concerned about fitting in, worried about *belonging*—and still struggled with abstract mathematical concepts.

When **Will** started sixth grade, he was somewhat socially immature and his physical appearance was similar to that of a fourth grader. And not much had changed by the end of the school year. But he was brilliant and could grasp a concept and fly with it before it had barely been presented. One Friday afternoon he asked, "What can you tell me about trigonometry?"

"Well, it has something to do with triangles," I answered.

On Monday morning he reported he'd read his dad's college trigonometry book; then he proceeded to give an overview of the field and ways trigonometry is used in the world.

Even though the boys were both 12 years old, they had vastly different developmental profiles, and if I wanted to help each of them (as well as all the other students in the classroom) *become* successful, I had to see each as a unique individual. If I had simply "taught to the middle," it would not have helped either of them feel as though he *belonged* among his peers.

John Swaim, a colleague of ours (who is also a former AMLE president and Lounsbury Award Honoree), devised a matrix for his Otterbein University pre-service and graduate students (many of them were middle level teachers) to help gain a better understanding of individual students. The matrix was a tool for plotting and getting an overview of different aspects of the individual's development.

The first step was to look at (and plot) the student's physical growth on the following scale: pre-pubescent (elementary student-like), early pubescent, pubescent, late pubescent, adolescent (adult-like).

The second step was to look at (and plot) cognitive growth or how a student might process information. This was examined on the following scale: pre-concrete, concrete, pre-abstract, abstract. Students at the concrete end of the spectrum tend to think more in the present and on the surface. Their thinking involves literal facts, ordinary sequences, and tangible objects. On the other end of the spectrum, abstract thinkers go beneath the surface to deal with ideas. Abstract thinking involves mental processes, understanding complex relationships, dealing with shades of gray, and making hypotheses and inferences.

If we were to place Kevin and Will on this matrix, it would be easy to see that Kevin fell on the high end of physical growth but more in the pre-concrete to concrete range cognitively. Will was the opposite—

early pubescent in physical growth; but cognitively, he was clearly an abstract thinker.

Wanting his students to delve deeper into understanding their students, Dr. Swaim added a third-dimension to the matrix and asked them to examine their students' social and psychological development based on their reasoning for making decisions. For this analysis, he adapted Lawrence Kohlberg's (1963) six stages of moral development. It is important to note that because these stages represent a flexible continuum of moral growth, at any given time young adolescents may move from one stage to another (including from a higher stage to a lower one) based on the decision being made and the circumstances surrounding it. Individual development was plotted on the matrix with a scale of Kohlberg's stages:

Pre-conventional:

1. Obedience and punishment

2. Self-interest and rewards

Conventional

3. Social approval

4. Authority and conformity to social order

Post-conventional:

5. Social contract

6. Universal ethics and internal moral principles

Admittedly, it would be difficult to analyze each student in such great detail. However, this is more than just an academic exercise. We see many benefits that can be gained when teachers do this kind of a process to look at individual students. We think you'll be amazed at what you learn when you take the time to ponder and record what you know about a student. The exercise will push you to find out things to which you hadn't paid enough attention! Try this—even if just with a few students to start. It will take you a long way toward seeing students not as a mass but as individuals. If time permits, it is valuable to repeat the review of a student's developmental characteristics later in the school year to observe changes.

Since a three-dimensional matrix can be cumbersome and since we realize that there are aspects of the individual's development (beyond the three mentioned) that teachers may want to examine, we've developed a modified approach to Dr. Swaim's process. Our adapted matrix, in the form of a table, gives teachers the flexibility to include other categories, use other scales, or describe students with observations rather than with a scale. See "Individual Development Profile," (Appendix B) on page 233 for a sample graphic worksheet that can be used to create individual profiles.

Yes, we must use the best research and information available to us to create conditions, programs, and lessons to help our students, as a group, to *belong* and *become*. But those plans have to make room for Kevin and Will and every other individual student. Each individual has his or her own unique set of features, needs, complications, assets, barriers, and skills in relatedness (*belonging*) and aspects of *becoming* (such as: autonomy, competence, and self-determination). Our plans and strategies can fit individuals within the group **only** when educators are competent at ascertaining where individuals are in different aspects of development.

As this chapter title states, a fundamental requirement for nurturing *belonging* and *becoming* is that middle level educators thoroughly understand young adolescent development. That is, if we don't truly "get" where our students are, right now, at their specific ages and stages, we might thwart, rather than nourish, their chances of *belonging* and *becoming* self-determined learners. All of our decisions about curriculum, instruction, assessment, school structure, programs, mission, and goals should be based on this rock solid foundation.

Putting It into Practice

As an individual, team, small group, or entire staff, use some of these activities to spark discussions, reflect on your current practices or situations, listen to others, or set goals.

1. Divide into groups according to the decade in which participants were 13 years old (those on the cusp of another decade can choose either decade). Ask them to draw a picture or make a list of what it was like to be 13 in their decade. What major events happened in the world? What was important to them? How did they dress? What music did they listen to, etc.? Share the pictures or lists, and then discuss how today's 13-year-olds are different than they were at 13. Then discuss how today's 13-year-olds are the same as they were when they were 13.

2. As a team, choose four or five students that you've found challenging to get to know or to reach. Use the Individual Development Profile (Appendix B) on page 234 to describe where you see those students falling in each of the categories. Share your results with each other, and look for areas of agreement and disagreement. Discuss how you might use that information to help each of those students increase in *belonging* or in an area of *becoming*.

3. Go to the website of the National Forum to Accelerate Middle-Grades Reform (www.mgforum.org), and download the free Schools to Watch Rubric. Individually complete the "Developmentally Responsive" section of the rubric. Tally the scores, and use the results as a springboard for a discussion on how developmentally responsive your school is to the needs of your students.

Chapter 3

Organize to Promote Belonging and Becoming

"Organizing is what you do before you do something, so that when you do it, it's not all mixed up."

- Winnie-the-Pooh

"If you don't know where you are going, you will end up somewhere else." No, Yogi Berra wasn't thinking about schools when he said this. But his axiom does remind us that the first step in becoming a quality middle level school is knowing and articulating where you are now and where you want to go. To become a reality, the larger school community must collaboratively build a vision around a set of core beliefs so that the vision becomes understood, expanded, nurtured, owned, and supported. And Winnie-the-Pooh is right; we've all experienced the "mixed-up-ness" of things (everything from one lesson to whole programs and structures) when someone didn't plan and organize well enough before getting started!

The organization of a school makes a difference for how the two foundational concepts *belonging* and *becoming* are embraced and addressed. Certain basic structures promote one or both of these processes; other structures inhibit them. For example, students are more likely to develop a sense of *belonging* and feel secure to develop many aspects of *becoming* in small, personalized learning environments (e.g., teams or advisory classes) than in the vast learning environment of the whole school. A smaller number of students assigned per teacher (i.e., 90 versus 120) helps teachers build relationships with students (*belonging* and *becoming*). Classroom arrangements where students can collaborate on tasks together increase both academic and personal growth (*becoming*) and positive relatedness (*belonging*). Academic settings with time and space for students to initiate learning, explore topics in depth, and experiment (as opposed to those with short, rigid time periods) give better chances for students to gain competence, autonomy, and knowledge (aspects of *becoming*). A schedule that provides time for teachers to collaborate as a staff or in grade-level groups or teams increases chances for true implementation of shared goals. Time dedicated to professional development enables teachers to grow in their abilities to understand developmental characteristics and to teach students skills they need for such things as self-determination, self-regulation, management of academic tasks (all are aspects of *becoming*), and *belonging*.

The conditions and structures we've described above are just some of the structures that affect student success, but all are features of an optimal middle level environment. We believe that the middle school concept is uniquely suited to offering conditions that help young adolescents *belong* and *become*.

Implementing the Middle School Concept

A good starting point for considering school organization and the benefits of the middle school concept is a review of the Association for Middle Level Education's landmark position statement on middle level education: *This We Believe: Keys to Educating Young Adolescents* (NMSA, 2010). This book builds a foundation for a school's design by defining four essential elements and 16 characteristics of a successful middle school. See Figure 3-1 for an overview of their design, "Successful Schools for Young Adolescents."

Figure 3-1

16 Characteristics

Curriculum, Instruction, and Assessment

Educators value young adolescents and are prepared to teach them. *Value Young Adolescents*

Students and teachers are engaged in active, purposeful learning. *Active Learning*

Curriculum is challenging, exploratory, integrative, and relevant. *Challenging Curriculum*

Educators use multiple learning and teaching approaches. *Multiple Learning Approaches*

Varied and ongoing assessments advance learning as well as measure it.
Varied Assessments

Leadership and Organization

A shared vision developed by all stakeholders guides every decision.
Shared Vision

Leaders are committed to and knowledgeable about this age group, educational research, and best practices. *Committed Leaders*

Leaders demonstrate courage and collaboration.
Courageous & Collaborative Leaders

Ongoing professional development reflects best educational practices.
Professional Development

Organizational structures foster purposeful learning and meaningful relationships. *Organizational Structures*

Culture and Community

The school environment is inviting, safe, inclusive, and supportive of all.
School Environment

Every student's academic and personal development is guided by an adult advocate. *Adult Advocate*

Comprehensive guidance and support services meet the needs of young adolescents. *Guidance Services*

Health and wellness are supported in curricula, school-wide programs, and related policies.
Health & Wellness

The school actively involves families in the education of their children. *Family Involvement*

The school includes community and business partners. *Community & Business*

Essential Attributes

An education for young adolescents must be

Developmentally Responsive
using the nature of young adolescents as the foundation on which all decisions are made.

Challenging
recognizing that every student can learn and everyone is held to high expectations.

Empowering
providing all students with the knowledge and skills they need to take control of their lives.

Equitable
advocating for every student's right to learn and providing challenging and relevant learning opportunities.

The Association for Middle Level Education

Successful Schools
for
Young Adolescents

What Makes Middle Schools Work (Wilcox, 2007), a research report from the State University of New York at Albany, offers further guidance. This project examined higher-performing middle level schools to look for common elements and practices. *Higher performing*, for the purposes of this study, was defined by the comparative level of academic performance of a school's students on New York State eighth-grade English language arts and mathematics assessments over a three-year period. The study concluded that the higher-performing middle schools had each built a culture of success by consistently maintaining five common elements. The study emphasizes that the elements are synergistic. Each one is important but cannot stand alone; they must all be implemented simultaneously. The identified elements are:

- **Trusting and Respectful Relationships**
  Relationships based on mutual trust and respect among administrators, teachers, students, and parents are fundamental to all of the common elements in the findings. Nurturing these relationships provides the backbone for successful learning.

- **Student's Social and Emotional Well-Being**
  Higher-performing schools recognize that creating a sense of security for middle school students provides them with a support network and a connection to their school, removing significant barriers to learning.

- **Teamwork**
  Higher-performing schools establish a collaborative environment and organizational structure that support teamwork between and among teachers, school leaders, and administrators. Groups of teachers, administrators, and specialists meet frequently and focus on specific instructional strategies and student performance within and across grades.

- **Evidence-based Decision-making**
  Sharing and using data from a variety of sources to make decisions is critical to helping schools achieve success. Data are frequently gathered, analyzed, and used in decision-making regarding the impacts of new programs, instructional practices, and interventions.

- **Shared Vision of Mission and Goals**
  When teachers and administrators build a vision of success and share goals, this leads to better communications, mutually agreed-upon expectations, and more long-term success (Wilcox, pp. 12-13).

If even one of the five elements is missing or lacking, it is far less likely that a middle level school will show high academic performance or that it will genuinely meet the needs of its students. These foundational elements are critical to ensuring that young adolescents have a place where they feel they *belong* so that they can develop positively in the many aspects of *becoming*.

There is no perfect way to organize a school. And there are no schedules that fit every school or every need.

Both of us have read, used, taught, and interacted with the two documents mentioned above many times over recent years. Now, since we've taken on the mindset that *belonging* and *becoming* are key foundations to the whole picture of what we believe young adolescents need, we can't help but notice the prominence (direct or inferred) of these two concepts in both resources! Look back at pages 37–39 and see if you don't have the same revelation!

Maintaining Flexibility

Certain structures, schedules, and factors of school organization certainly contribute to students' well-being in a range of areas. Yet what matters even more than the specific details is what happens within the organization. Ron Williamson (2009), author of "The Schedule as a Tool to Improve Student Learning," explained:

> There is no perfect way to organize a school. And there are no schedules that fit every school or every need. What's clear, however, is that the way you organize your school is a reflec-

tion of your school's values and priorities and can either support achieving your vision or become a barrier to its success. Without a clear vision and agreed upon goals, the schedule is merely a plan for organizing teachers and students. But when guided by goals the schedule becomes a powerful tool to positively impact teaching and learning (p. 4).

The best organization for middle level schools has long been considered to center around interdisciplinary teams within a flexible schedule that also includes a built-in advisory time. For a variety of reasons, at my former school, my staff and I (Patti) were unable to implement this type of a structure. But we still wanted to create a framework that addressed the needs of young adolescents. After trying a few variations, we created a structure in which each student was placed on two teams—one for language arts and social studies and a second for math, science, and health. Teams were multi-age, and students generally stayed on the same teams for more than one year.

We knew this was not the "ideal" organization for a middle school, so the staff continued to explore ways to move to complete interdisciplinary teaming. We had the good fortune to enjoy a visit from Dr. Paul George, a noted middle level scholar and author. He spent a day at the school to look at and give feedback on our program. In his summary report, he described the school's structure as "fresh, different, and effective." He felt the organization was a "workable alternative to traditional interdisciplinary team organization [and that] it [would] be hard to improve upon the attention individual students receive in this arrangement."

Because the staff had kept the focus on creating an effective school for the students, we were able to think outside of the norm to create an organizational structure that worked for the school. Teachers valued this feedback, appreciated that having an organizational structure that benefitted students didn't mean having to adopt a "canned" program, and were reaffirmed that they were doing what was best for the students.

The multi-year structure provided additional support for students from adults they knew and trusted. It gave them a sense of security and allowed them to be themselves while having a place to *belong*. Once students felt comfortable and had a sense of *belonging* at the school, they were more able to *become* academically and personally successful. We repeat Ron Williamson's caution: there is no one schedule or organizational structure that works for all schools. The schedule described above was difficult to create and challenging to implement; it worked because it was designed around the school's specific needs and resources. It was risky, required thinking "outside of the box," and might be hard to replicate.

Sadly, the check-off mentality is still alive in middle schools today. Elements such as flexible block schedules, shared students, common planning time, proximity of classrooms, and student advisory are still considered by many to be required components of an effective middle school. Some even suggest that a school can't practice a middle level concept unless these components are present. And while those structures are good and have been proven to be effective, it's far too easy for a school to check them off the list and then believe that they have created a school where students feel they *belong* and can *become* all they are meant to be.

But that's not the case. A school may have integrated teams with common planning time, but all the teachers talk about in team meetings is student behavior—never about how to connect their curriculum and instruction, develop and consistently use common protocols, or pursue professional development as a team. The school may have a schedule that can be flexed, but all class periods remain the same length of time, month after month, year after year. An advisory period may be present but used as a time to work on homework and do school "business" rather than addressing social, emotional, psychological, and cognitive issues and needs. Structure in and of itself does not guarantee an effective middle school.

Sustaining Middle Level Practices in Times of Change

There is no question that dwindling resources combined with more stringent accountability standards have had significant impacts on middle level schools across the country. In most locations, educators and school boards grapple with such realities as reductions in staff levels, pressures to increase instructional time in reading and math, and shrinking budgets. These have led many schools to move away from established middle level structures that included advisory periods, teaming, individual and team prep time, and block schedules.

Yet when faced with this dilemma, some schools rise to the challenge and look for creative ways to keep the middle school concept alive, regardless of the constraints of a less-than-ideal schedule (or budget). The first step in accomplishing this is to determine the "why" of structures such as teaming, advisory, flexible schedules, exploratory classes, and others. For example, here are possible outcomes for common middle level structures.

Structure	Outcome

- **Teaming** allows for smaller and more personalized learning communities.

- **Advisory classes** contribute to building relationships and belonging.

- **Block schedules** provide opportunity for flexibility in learning practices.

- **Common planning time** makes it possible for teachers to collaborate.

- **Interdisciplinary organization** facilitates connections between subject areas.

- **Elective classes** increase student exposure and exploration within different topics.

- **Team-leader council** builds collaborative leadership.

Once staff members agree on the purposes of these structures, it's possible to think creatively to find ways to meet those needs that do not rely on a particular structure. To help with this process, schools must first clarify what they are trying to accomplish. For example, are you compensating for loss of staff? Looking for ways to reduce expenditures? Trying to provide additional instruction time in a content area? Be sure you don't fall into the trap of "we've always done it this way." We visited one middle school where staff members were able to accomplish their goals once they realized that not every class had to meet every day for the same amount of time and that teachers did not have to have the same prep period every day.

When a middle school team in North Carolina was faced with the loss of their advisory period, team members decided that the benefits of the program were far too important to abandon. So they searched for ways to infuse advisory activities throughout the day. The team's advisory program had been built around 12 character traits and actions that formed the basis for their team's core values. Because the team strongly believed in the importance of the program, each teacher committed to using 10 to 15 minutes of class time three days a month in order to introduce the concepts to the students. They continued to infuse this program into all aspects of classroom and team meetings, classroom discussions, reflections when behavioral issues arose, goal setting for conference time, recognizing and celebrating individual accomplishments, and more. This team, convinced that the well-being of each child is at the core of what good middle schools do, was not about to use the loss of advisory classes as a reason to abandon this belief. Instead, they put their heads together and launched an alternative plan to assure the same benefits were still available to their students.

Here's one caution: Changes in a school's program can evoke strong emotions from a variety of sources. Be sure that any process to create or modify a school's organizational structure is collaborative and inclusive. Gather thoughts and suggestions from a variety of stakeholders, including students.

To design a school structure that best furthers the processes of *belonging* and *becoming*, follow the advice of the sixth AMLE characteristic of successful schools for young adolescents (see page 37), the fifth element of the *What Makes Middle Schools Work* report (see page 39), and Yogi Berra (see page 35): start with a shared vision of what those processes are, what your beliefs are, and what you want to happen for students. Next, take seriously the reality of how your school's structure affects its ability to meet the academic and developmental needs of your students. Then, after asking "How can we meet our goals for students in ways that satisfy our vision and beliefs?" agree on what to do. Identify the kinds of specific programs or classes that will focus on strategies for *becoming* and *belonging* while keeping a balance with a strong focus on academic learning. Set programs and schedules that can reasonably lead to meeting your goals and addressing your students' needs.

After your plans are underway, don't forget to keep reexamining the structure. Don't shy away from being flexible enough to make needed adjustments to the structure over time or to completely revamp it. And even when you're forced to lose or change part of the structure, be creative enough to find ways to ensure the outcomes you believe to be critical for your students.

Putting It into Practice

As an individual, team, small group, or entire staff, use some of these activities to spark discussions, reflect on your current practices or situations, listen to others, or set goals.

1. As a group, examine and discuss AMLE's list of attributes and characteristics of a successful school shown on page 37. What evidence can you give that some or all of these elements and characteristics are implemented in your school? Which do you see as your strongest areas? What areas need improvement?

2. Questions for group discussion: What do you see as the structural elements of an "ideal" middle level school? Which are in place at your school? Are they effective? Which are missing or could be improved? Are there elements at your school that are implemented in name only? Do areas need more flexibility? Have you given up important aspects that need to be reconsidered using a more flexible method?

3. Examine the list of structures and outcomes on page 42. Do you agree with the outcomes for each structure? What would you change? How do you address ones that are missing?

4. Go to the website of the National Forum to Accelerate Middle-Grades Reform (www.mgforum.org), and download the Schools to Watch Rubric. Individually complete the "Organizational Structures and Processes" section of the rubric. Tally the scores, and use the results as a springboard for a discussion on how your school meets the criteria.

PART II
Practices for
Belonging and Becoming

Once a strong foundation is laid, it's time to build the rest of the house. With that process come multiple decisions that make each structure unique. Each school will choose (and decide how to implement) policies, practices, and programs to promote *belonging* and *becoming*. Some decisions will be influenced by codes and legal requirements; but for all decisions that are within the control of the staff and other stakeholders, start from the base of your school's shared mission, beliefs, vision, and goals. Though the environment you shape for your students to *belong* and *become* may be patterned after other successful models, it must depend heavily on the needs, preferences, and characteristics of **your** students, staff, parents, and community. No two schools are exactly alike. The choices for your school will work only if they address your unique situation. Don't feel pressured to be a mirror image of someone else's school.

In Part II, we share practical strategies and examples to help students experience their schools as places where they can *belong* and *become*. The chapters offer suggestions for creating and sustaining the conditions and skills that cultivate various aspects of those processes through

1. Creating a culture of connection throughout the school.
2. Believing in students.
3. Fostering academic competence and autonomy.
4. Facilitating personal development, including self-determination and self-regulation.
5. Inviting, hearing, and nurturing students' voices in the school.
6. Offering students many choices in all aspects of their school lives.
7. Teaching leadership skills and providing leadership opportunities for all students.
8. Celebrating students' successes at *belonging* and *becoming*.

Chapter 4

Create Connections and Community

"No significant learning occurs without a significant relationship."
- Dr. James Comer

Many young teachers, particularly at the middle and high school levels, enter the education field believing they've been hired to teach a specific subject. They are often passionate, eager, ready to change the world—in short, holding those attitudes we hope to find in beginning teachers! But the idea that any teacher is hired to teach a specific subject is not quite right; he or she was hired to teach students. And there is a difference between the two. Certainly a school needs capable, skilled teachers with strong preparations for their content backgrounds. But all practitioners must realize that students' sense of well-being and experience of connectedness (*belonging*) influences everything else we hope for them to be, accomplish, and *become*.

What do we mean by *community*? Sociologist Karen Osterman (2000), who has spent many years researching and teaching in the areas of *belonging* in the school community, defined it this way:

A community exists when its members experience a sense of belonging or personal relatedness. In a community, the members feel that the group is important to them and that they are important to the group. Members of a community feel that the group will satisfy their needs: they will be cared for and supported. Finally, the community has a shared and emotional sense of connection (p. 324).

In Chapter 1, we outlined many of the critical benefits of *belonging* along with some effects of not *belonging*. Osterman concluded from her research that, sadly, many schools still pay little attention to students' social and psychological needs, have structures or practices that contribute to isolation or alienation for some students, operate on beliefs that academic achievement is more important than needs for relatedness, or have a pervasive attitude that *belonging* is a "reward for compliance and achievement" rather than a "precondition for engagement" (p. 324).

The good news is this: research shows that instructional practices and aspects of school climate—even short programs focused on *belonging*—can help students feel accepted in their school and classrooms; they can also "acknowledge and normalize students' worries about *belonging* and explain how these concerns can lessen with time" (Romero, 2015, pp. 3-4). In addition, efforts to build community in a school lead to increased academic motivation, social and emotional competencies, and lowered rates of violence—all aspects of the kinds of *becoming* we wish for our students (Schaps, 2003). A note of caution: When designing specific practices and programs to increase *belonging*, take care to reach the *belonging* needs of all students. It is critical to realize "that an increased sense of *belonging* for some students at the exclusion of other students may lead to detrimental outcomes for some students, such as greater levels of perceived social rejection and greater reports of problems at school (Anderman, 2002, p. 807).

> **Even short programs focused on belonging—can help students feel accepted in their school and classrooms.**

Shaping the Community

Being aware of the meaning and benefits of *community* is just the first step. Beyond that: **All school personnel** must share in the belief that success for students includes social and emotional well-being in addition to (and with as much importance as) academic well-being. **All students** must participate in planned experiences that focus on community—in their schools and in their classrooms. **All staff members** (and volunteers) in the school must put efforts into developing the culture that helps students feel included, important, and safe. **All parents, guardians, and family members** must hear the message about the importance of social and emotional well-being in combination with reaching academic goals. They must consistently be invited to be involved in creating this supportive community.

Even though we don't have control over such things as state mandates and district budgets, many of the programs, strategies, and attitudes that build the kind of community middle level schools need **are** within the control of educators. And many of them do not involve budget increases or more staffing! Based on evidence from current research, the most effective practices and conditions for helping students feel connected to their school include

- Active creation of trusting, caring relationships among students, teachers, school staff, and students' families.
- Whole-school, concerted efforts to ensure students' physical and psychological safety.
- Common values and practices across the school focused on such qualities as respect, care for others, cooperation, personal responsibility, and good character.
- Teaching and reinforcing of social and emotional skills.
- Commitment to (and expectations of) respect for everyone and from everyone.
- Removal of any roadblocks to learning while offering academic support to all students.

- Frequent opportunities for students to develop and exercise autonomy—including taking part in school situations where they make or influence decisions.
- Equity in expectations for and in treatment of all students; visible respect for differences.
- Intentional strategies to ensure that every student feels close to and known by at least one adult in the school.
- Regular opportunities for students to cooperate and collaborate with one another.
- Intentional, planned conversations between the school (staff and students) and parents and school-wide community-building events that connect the school with students' families.
- Professional development in *belonging*, social and emotional well-being, and interpersonal skills (Anderman, 2002; Centers for Disease Control and Prevention, 2009; Furrer and Skinner, 2003; Henderson & Mapp, 2002; Osterman, 2000; Romero, 2015; Battistich, Solomon, Watson, & Schaps, 1997; Schaps, Battistich, & Solomon, 2003; Wingspread, 2004).

Building Relationships

At the end of my (Laurie's) daughter's fifth-grade year in middle school, parents were informed that all sixth-grade students would be required to take either band or orchestra as a full-year, every-other-day class. Emma was asked to choose an instrument. I'm a strong supporter of music education and its impact on student achievement. However, as a family we struggled with her having to take a class that required a good deal of at-home practice because she was already committed to many other out-of-school activities. But, it was just for one year, and we knew it would be good for her, so (somewhat begrudgingly) we rented her a viola for the next year.

Throughout sixth grade, there was rarely a week that Emma didn't have a story to share about her orchestra teacher. Emma loved how the teacher taught class, how she involved students, and how she made her feel special. When Emma was honored with the monthly orchestra award, it was as if she had won the World Cup. When her class performed its Christmas concert, my husband and I were amazed at how much she enjoyed playing and how beautifully her peers played together.

At the end of the year when it was time to return the rented viola, Emma informed us that she would need to purchase a new, larger one, because she was choosing to take orchestra as a daily year-long class in seventh grade. She saw our surprise—after all, it had been a bit of a fight to get her on board for the obligatory sixth-grade year. She remarked simply, "I have to be in her class. I don't care what she teaches." Though the initial class was a requirement (and might not have been Emma's choice originally), the relationship she developed with her teacher made all the difference. As a result, we now have a viola player in the family!

Outside of their families, schools provide the most important set of relationships that young adolescents can experience; there are so many possibilities for relationships within small and large groups. School is the ideal place—if the climate is right—for developing healthy relationships and a sense of *belonging* (O'Brien & Bowles, 2013).

Relationships within a school form the cornerstones for a culture of trust and respect where students want to *belong* and meet the expectations in their school. If we want students to believe they are valued, respected members of the school community and that the school has been designed to meet their needs as they grow and develop—then we must believe it, too, and show that it is true. This belief must actively and constantly pervade the atmosphere of the school.

Teacher-Student Relationships

Teachers who form secure, meaningful relationships with students share these characteristics: They are warm, caring, sensitive, and affirming. They are attentive and emotionally available to students.

They are trustworthy, fair, equitable, and consistent. Students can rely on them to be even tempered. They don't yell or threaten. They don't alienate students by embarrassing or belittling them or shame students by lecturing them about their shortcomings or misdoings. They don't discipline or scold one student in front of others; they confront students in private and give them a way to save face in front of their peers. They do not show biases or favoritism. They're honest and direct and not afraid to enjoy and use humor. They set high standards and help students reach them. They affirm students' efforts and talents; they honor each student's unique qualities. They are obvious and passionate advocates for students. Students notice that these teachers enjoy their students and work hard to help every student succeed. These teachers treat all students with respect at all times.

There is no precise relationship formula that works with every student. Middle level students come in all shapes and sizes and have their own unique stories to tell that bear hearing. We must take the time to listen and look beneath the surface. Otherwise we'll fail at truly understanding that student; we won't be able to build an authentic relationship. When we pay close attention, we'll learn things we didn't know; for example, The boy with hair dyed black and wearing baggy clothing is one of the school's honor students. The girl sitting in the corner of the room and not saying much delivers food to the homeless in the park on weekends. The popular girl chatting animatedly with her friends battles an eating disorder. The boy being reprimanded for his third tardy takes responsibility for getting his younger brothers and sisters off to school each morning.

When we pay close attention, we'll learn things we didn't know.

Are we expecting Sasha to be as academically proficient as her older sister? Do we think "Jeff's doing the best he can given his home life?" Do we unintentionally favor Bella because her mother is head of the

PTA? Do we have a preconceived notion of Curt's behavior because of what we were told by his last year's teacher? Do we make judgments about Jenna because of rumors we hear about her out-of-school relationships with boys? We must get beyond our first impressions and face any prejudices we may have, especially those that may be hidden.

Even when a student doesn't initially show an interest in establishing a relationship with a teacher, it's the teacher's responsibility to take the lead. Middle level speaker and author Rick Wormeli (2010) cautions teachers not to put the responsibility for a teacher-student relationship onto the student. He says: "A lot of teachers hide behind that 50/50 notion. Like the kid has to meet me halfway. No! After 25 years of teaching, it's much more 60/40, and the one kid who sits in the back of the room and never interacts, 90/10" (2:18).

Skilled educators know (and research supports) the value of having caring relationships with students: classroom disruptions are minimized, engagement in learning increases, and students *become* more successful in a variety of academic and personal aspects (Martin & Dowson, 2009; Rimm-Kaufman & Sandilos, 2011). The teacher's positive, consistent, friendly attention to their needs and concerns gains their trust and increases students' senses of *belonging*.

Teacher Relationships with Others

Young adolescent students may appear to be disinterested in the adults in the school. But make no mistake, they are always watching! They notice what the teachers and other adults do. They notice how you talk to and treat other students. They notice your attitudes and preferences. They are keenly aware of your facial expressions and body language. They notice how you relate to your colleagues. They notice how your voice changes when a parent enters the room. They notice when you roll your eyes about something another teacher says or does. They overhear your conversations.

The relationship behaviors of adults are perhaps the most powerful lessons for students. Intentionally or not, all the adults in the school are models for how to carry out relationships—how to treat others, how to be trustworthy and loyal, how to handle conflicts and frustrations, and how to handle one's own emotions in relationships. To be secure in their relationships at school, students must see the adults around them operating with the care, respect, compassion, and control that we try to teach to them.

Student-Student Relationships

As all middle level educators well know, relationships among students play a large part in individual well-being at school. Yes, the teacher-student relationship is powerful and sets a model for young adolescents to emulate. But how their peers see and interact with them is what middle level students notice and worry about the most. Students can truly feel they *belong* **only** when they are at ease with both the adults and other students in their school.

Heather Libbey's (2004) analysis of school connectedness found peer relations to be a key component of *belonging*. The benefits gained from trusting teacher-student relationships extend and multiply when students feel they *belong* with peers. In their overview of research on the effects of student relatedness at school, Furrer and Skinner (2003) report that peers are a potent influence on students' self-concept, educational goals, and day-to-day behaviors and satisfaction at school. Allen and Bowles (2012) concluded that social *belonging* positively affects classroom engagement, student motivation, and academic performance. Fostering healthy relationships among students is a critical part of the teacher's role. Here are some ways to do that:

- First and foremost (at the risk of sounding repetitive)— **model** caring, respectful relationships.

- By your actions and reactions, show that you honor differences and appreciate the uniqueness of each individual.

- Set strong expectations for students respecting one another, and hold them to it.

- Give students responsibilities for increasing *belonging* in the class. Let them make and implement plans to do this.

- Define *respect*. Define *disrespect*. Talk about these with students. Let them give examples of what both of these look like in action. Get them talking about what it feels like to be the recipient of respect, disrespect, disregard (or ignoring), esteem, and value.

- Notice and celebrate examples of respectful, caring, and uplifting behaviors.

- Do not ignore incidents of disrespect (of any magnitude).

- Teach students skills of actively and respectfully listening to each other.

- Teach students to give respectful, useful input and responses to each other.

- Get students involved in lots of interactive activities—cooperative problem solving, group discussions, joint research, and group projects.

- Mix up groups so that students dialogue and work with everyone in the class.

- Give meaningful tasks that enable students to succeed at group efforts.

- Plan opportunities for peer tutoring.

- Constantly validate students' opinions, ideas, and feelings.

- Ask for input from all students. Honor the input you receive.

- Help all students succeed. Let their peers see their successes.

- Find opportunities to showcase each student's skills, interests, and competence.

- Teach and practice such interpersonal skills as communication, listening, decision-making, self-control, and conflict resolution.

- Emphasize and practice pro-social behavior (students helping others).

- Emphasize and practice non-exclusionary attitudes. Let students identify what these are and discuss behaviors that show evidence of non-exclusion.

I (Patti) am reminded of a group of about five girls in my sixth grade class who were having a conflict that seemed never-ending. (Anyone who has worked with middle level girls who are having "friendship issues" knows that it can be a treacherous experience.) Finally, I decided to meet with the group to see if the problems could be settled once and for all. I asked each of them to state the issue in her own words. Then I gave them the standard teacher "chat" on getting along, forgiving and forgetting, etc.—a lecture I'm sure we've all used a few times. At the end, there was silence. Then Heather spoke up: "So what you're telling us is that we don't have to be friends, but we do have to be friendly. I think we can do that." Heads nodded; conflict resolved! (And, in the manner of sixth grade girls, they were all friends a week later!)

Making Individual Connections

This chapter is about building a connected environment; and as we've emphasized, there are a host of practices that schools and individuals in it can do to foster connectedness for all students. But here's the thing: We can't connect to students we don't know. We can't be models of connection if students don't see us getting to know them

> **We can't connect to students we don't know.**

and other students—not just knowing on the surface but knowing and valuing what's inside. So make a commitment to getting to know students as individuals. Find out what's important to them. Hold conversations with them about their out-of-school interests. Notice what drives and inspires them. Pay attention to what discourages them. Discover what's on their minds, and they will begin to see you as someone who is genuinely interested in them. It's like looking for the prize in the box of Cracker Jack—you know it's in there somewhere!

Finding out (and honoring) what students value is a strong component of getting to know students. Teachers need to be tuned in to the interests and activities of the whole group of young adolescents. This means paying attention to the fads, fashions, events, heroes, music, media, games, and activities that—yes—consume their time and energies. But to know students more deeply, we must also hone in on the particular passions of individuals.

From my time as a middle school principal, I (Laurie) remember a student who really struggled in one teacher's class. (In fairness, he struggled in all of his classes, but his other teachers had found some common ground and were able to help Michael make some progress). But in this one class, he and the teacher just couldn't seem to connect. Looking for something to break this cycle, the teacher stayed after school to watch Michael play in a school basketball game. He cheered this talented player on (although not so obviously that it would embarrass the student). The next day in class, he used something from Michael's basketball performance as an example of a lesson concept. From then on, it was almost as if they had never had a problem (and they had very few after that)! Michael got a message that the teacher valued this very important part of his life. As a result, he was more open to the values the teacher was trying to teach (a win-win for both—but mostly for Michael).

What we adults see as important in education may not hold the same significance for our students. Whether or not our values jibe with theirs, our goal is to reach and educate the whole student. So we must recognize the parts of their lives that are as important to them as (or possibly—more important than) academics: school-sponsored or out-of-school arts, athletics, clubs, volunteer activities, family responsibilities—or even jobs. We must also recognize that their participation in the ventures they value can have a major impact on their academic achievement. When we honor what they value and show our enthusiasm, we deepen trusting relationships with individuals. These relationships, in turn, make it more possible for us to contribute to shaping other values related to aspects of *becoming* productive, well-rounded learners and citizens. So it's good for each of us to ask ourselves: "Do I see math class, cheerleading practice, working for a skateboard competition, being a part of the football team, building a babysitting business, helping clean up the city park, writing songs for a garage band, coding a video game, and scoring well on a state science test **all** as equally important for students?"

You might be thinking, "We all know it's critical to build relationships with students. I want to get to know my students individually, but I have so many students! How can I do this?" First of all, realize that you may know more about individuals than you think. Take the time to make a quick list of what you do know about each student. Start this early in the year, and jot down other things as you learn them. Plan some quick activities (such as those below) that help you learn more in a short amount of time. Learn more things about students from teammates or other adults who work with them. Then, make brief "check-in" contacts with each student at least once a week—find time to make a comment about something you know or have observed about him or her, follow up on something the student has shared, or encourage one of the student's interests or ventures.

Here are some strategies you might try to get to know individual students more closely:

"About Me" Letters—Ask students to write you a letter telling what they think you should know about them.

Student Inventories—To get a close-up look at individuals, ask students to share likes, dislikes, hobbies, interests, and personality traits.

They can complete such sentences as:

What I value most is . . .

My most burning interest is . . .

What teachers usually don't know about me is . . .

I prefer to spend my time . . .

I'm really good at . . .

Something fascinating about me is . . .

I worry about . . .

I'm proud of . . .

My biggest concern at school is . . .

Get-to-Know-Me Lists—Ask students to make such lists as: My Top Ten Interests, My Top Ten Hopes, Ten Words That Tell About Me, Top Five Ways I Learn Best and Five Things That Keep Me From Learning, Five Things I Wish Would Happen at School, etc.

Parent Input—Give parents ways to tell what they'd like you to know about their child, what they're proud of, and what they hope will happen for their child at school this year. These might take the form of letters, surveys, student interviews with parents, questionnaires—or even just sentences on note cards.

Extracurricular Activity Check-Ups—Investigate the extracurricular involvement of each student in your class. Every student in a middle school should have some outside activity as a chance to pursue an interest and interact with more peers in satisfying experiences. If you find the student has no such involvement, work with him or her to find the right activity. (This should be done throughout the school so that every student has a chance for connections beyond his classes. It can only work if the school offers some opportunities during the school day so there will be no reason why a student can't participate.)

Visits to Students' Events—Drop in on events students care about—sports games, concerts, debates, recitals, clubs, and other places they share their talents. Even if the student is not a performer in an event, you can show your interest in what she or he values by showing up to see what it's all about. A nice side benefit of attending events is that you have more chances to engage with parents—who often attend events to support their children's interests. Being a part of an event shows parents that you believe in the non-academic participation and support what the student values. This strengthens your relationship with both student and parents.

Building positive connections with individuals is like depositing money in the bank. If the time comes when you have to confront a student or get to the hard stuff of dealing with a big problem, you want to be sure there is "money" in the account to withdraw. You'll already have established the trust that helps them believe you are their advocate.

Ensuring That Each Student Is Known

In most cases, middle level teachers have dozens of students rotating through their classrooms in a day. Even when each teacher is doing her or his best to know each student, individual students at this level might not feel closely connected to or completely secure with any one adult. A student may not know where to turn for a consistent listener or advocate. To give our students the best chance to *belong* and *become*, we must ensure that every student is well

To give our students the best chance to belong and become, we must ensure that every student is well known and feels close to at least one adult in the school and preferably more than one.

known and feels close to at least one adult in the school and preferably more than one (Carnegie Council on Adolescent Development, 1989, 1995; Wingspread, 2004). That adult does not necessarily have to be a teacher. He or she could be the custodian, a secretary, a classroom paraprofessional, a lunchroom worker, the principal, a counselor, the librarian or media specialist—any caring adult who can connect with the student and who takes responsibility for being that child's advocate. This adult is alert to the student's successes and struggles, tuned in to whether or not the student has a sense of *belonging* and how the student perceives her or his progress and abilities in the personal and academic processes of *becoming*. The advocate can connect the student with services, programs, other adults, other students, organizations, and opportunities that can enhance the progress or address the needs.

A school organization that includes teaming and advisory classes has long been considered an indicator of an effective middle school. A deeper look into the "why" reveals that these practices diminish anonymity. No student should feel lost or anonymous, particularly not during the difficult time of adolescence. Teaming creates smaller learning communities, and advisories help develop strong student-adult and student-student connections. If your school is not able to implement teaming and advisory programs, it's important to look for other strategies to fill the same functions for creating the culture of connectedness in the school.

At the middle school where I (Patti) was principal, we did not have a formal advisory program. Yet the staff knew the importance of ensuring that each student was closely connected with at least one adult. So, on the wall of the staff room, we posted a list of all our students. All school employees (not just teachers) were asked to read over the list and star names of students with whom they had a strong, personal relationship (for example, the student would initiate conversations, the adult knew the family, or the adult had a connection with the student in some extracurricular activity). In addition, each adult put a checkmark by the names of students with whom they felt they had some relationship (but not as strong as those they had starred). After everyone had left stars and checkmarks, a group of us examined the list. (It was interesting that those with the most markings by their names tended to be the "top" students and the "disruptive" students.)

Unfortunately, there were student names with no stars or checks. The staff read through the list of those without marks, and individuals stepped forward to commit to developing a relationship with one or more of those students. Generally, it was along the lines of "Oh, she's in my second period class; I'll make a point to speak with her each day" or "I see him sitting by himself at lunch each day. I can ask him if he'd help me with something."

As principal, I remember one student I had chosen. I made sure to initiate a conversation with him several times a week while doing lunch duty. It was my last year as principal, and the following year I received a wrong-number phone call from the student's father. I recognized the name on the caller ID and told him that I'd been his son's principal. He immediately told me how much his son missed me because I was "really nice" and "talked with him a lot!"

This process was an effective way to find out about our students' connections to adults in the building and to make a change for those who did not have a clear adult advocate. It also served as a good reminder to staff about just how important it is to reach out to all students.

Respecting Differences

Schools are centers of diversity—in things related to race, ethnicity, religion, language, capabilities, cultural patterns and values, and sexual orientation or identification. As we work to forge a connected school community, we must remember and respect the differences among us. This means that we must examine our own

Student responses to differences can become roadblocks to a sense of belonging for other students.

attitudes about and responses to differences, teach our students to value differences, and require behaviors that show acceptance and respect.

Unfortunately, student responses to differences can become roadblocks to a sense of *belonging* for other students. At the middle grades level, in addition to the diversity factors listed above, a host of physical, emotional, social, and personal-choice differences distinguishes students and can lead to more stereotyping, mocking, exclusion, or criticism. These include such things as weight, height, body type, emotional vulnerability (someone who cries easily), sound of voice, hair style or color, clothing choices, friend choices, popularity (or lack thereof), activities engaged in (or not engaged in), or even just being new to the school. An 11-year-old girl feels ostracized if she isn't included in a "cool" or "popular" peer group or clique. For an unathletic 13-year-old boy, not making the basketball team can be a devastating exclusion from a group to which he so desperately wants to *belong*.

As middle level educators, we must watch for such instances. We can help connect the 11-year-old girls with other friends, and we can structure athletic programs to be inclusive with opportunities for all students to participate. We can establish an environment where students understand that differences are part of the human race— where they feel they *belong* as whole persons because of who they are.

Researchers Battistich, Solomon, and colleagues (1995, 1997) conducted a long-term intervention to create a sense of community in schools. Outcomes of this project (known as the Child Development Project) led them to believe that promotion of non-exclusionary attitudes was one of the key ways to increase a sense of *belonging* among students. We must help students identify exclusion and inclusion, understand the importance of inclusion, and practice behaviors that show inclusion. Whether there is a new sixth grader sitting alone at lunch with no friends, an eighth grader of a different religion who feels uncomfortable during a seemingly harmless discussion about Christmas in the hallway, or a fifth grader who feels excluded due to his race, a critical part of our role as educators is helping guide students through what it means to see life from someone else's perspective and to honor all humans equally.

How well we do (or don't do) in teaching the life lessons of respect and inclusion will make a difference in whether students can realize that actions they see as innocent, light-hearted jokes or gestures may be felt by others as demeaning, harassing, or bullying. Here are a few of many possible ways to help students embrace and honor diversity:

- Define *diversity, stereotype, inclusion, tolerance, intolerance,* and *worth.* Discuss these. Have students offer examples of these (without using names).

- Together, brainstorm, discuss, and role-play ways to show inclusion in the school community.

- Encourage and practice open-mindedness about people who look, act, celebrate, or think differently from themselves.

- Watch yourself and listen to yourself! Examine your own attitudes and (even subtle) manifestations of bias, prejudice, exclusion, or stereotyping. Work with colleagues to reflect these to each other. Know that your students will pick these up! Show, by your behavior, what it looks like to embrace and celebrate differences.

- Notice external messages that students see and hear—from media and other sources in society. Teach students to be alert to these. Teach skills for evaluating and responding to these.

- Help to organize and participate in professional development to further equity and inclusive behaviors in your school.

- Make sure the stories you read, activities you do, lessons you plan, foods you share, units you cover, field trips you take, and art you show are deliberately chosen to expose students to many cultures.

- Have students explore and share their own cultural histories, values, and traditions.

- Encourage students to try to put themselves in another person's shoes.

- Discuss courage as it relates to standing up to prejudice, intolerance, or exclusion.

Including and Collaborating with Parents

The African proverb "It takes a whole village to raise a child" is certainly true in middle schools. If we want to create schools where students *belong* and can develop their potential for many of the qualities of *becoming*, we must have the help and support of parents. Research has repeatedly confirmed what educators know from experience: Parent involvement and support makes a difference for students!

Studies have found that students with involved parents, no matter what their income or background, are more likely to

- Earn higher grades and test scores.
- Be promoted, pass their classes, and earn credits.
- Attend school regularly.
- Have better social skills, show improved behavior, and adapt well to school.
- Graduate and go on to postsecondary education. (Ferguson, 2009, Sec. 2, p. 7)

The above list shows some of the qualities, habits, efforts, and attitudes that are a part of our own lists of what we want students to *become*. Ongoing, positive relationships between teachers and families greatly boost a student's sense of *belonging* as well. Imagine the messages you send to a student about "having his back" or being her advocate when you reach out to affirm that student to the parents. (And be sure that most of your contacts with parents **are** for the purpose of reporting progress, improvements, compliments, and other positive messages!)

Unfortunately, many parents feel a need to back off from school involvement during the middle years (and yes, that decision is often instigated or supported by their child). Other parents do not recall their days at the middle level fondly and do not care to revisit them by coming to school. Still others avoid the school because of language or culture issues.

It's great to have parents participate in groups such as a PTA or PTO, help with fundraisers or carnivals, or serve on short-term committees. Yet, if we truly want to make schools places where students feel they *belong* and where they can *become* what they want now and in the future, we must work to develop deeper partnerships with parents. This begins each year with establishment of a strong two-way communication process.

- Make positive contacts with each student's family at the beginning of the year. Tell them something you value about their child. (This shows that you have already made an effort to get to know the child as an individual.)

- Set up a workable system to keep parents well informed about classroom procedures, events, and homework.

- Set up a consistent way to communicate with parents. Find out what is the best way for them to receive information or make contact.

- Be accessible. Let them know how to reach you. Be sure to find ways to accommodate language differences. Respond quickly to any attempts parents make to contact you.

- Keep in regular contact with parents about the accomplishments, progress, and needs of their child.

- Compliment each student to his or her parents several times a year—with a note, email, or call that is only for the purpose of telling something positive.

- Always be warm, kind, and respectful to students' families. Ask parents for their ideas and concerns. Listen to what they tell you. (Listen as much as you talk—or more.)

- Whenever there is a problem or concern, contact parents personally (phone or face-to-face) and make a plan together. (We encourage you not to use email to share concerns. It may be quicker, but it is often far less personal and effective. It is difficult to interpret tone, and you can unintentionally send the wrong message—making the situation worse, not better.) Always follow up to discuss how the plan is working and to give affirmations of the student.

To further build authentic connections with parents that support *belonging* and *becoming*, explore additional ways to engage them. It's wonderful when parents initiate involvement with school. But it's our role to reach out to them—to see that there are intentional practices that offer numerous and creative ways for parents to support their child's learning experience. Teachers and school administrators should ask questions such as these:

> "Are parents fully functioning members of the school's leadership council?"

> "Does the school regularly seek feedback on current policies and practices?"

> "Has the school taken the opportunity of a school event (such as a concert, movie night, or sports activity) to intersperse a short informational talk about how parents can support their children at home?"

> "Does the school hold transition meetings for incoming students? (If there are multiple feeder schools, have we considered holding the meetings at their neighborhood school?)"

> "Do parents who do not speak English feel comfortable at our school?"

A powerful way to engage parents is through student-led conferences, a process that has parents coming to school to hear students sharing a portfolio of classroom work samples, articulating strengths and weaknesses, and using a goal-setting process for future accomplishments. This kind of conference makes significant contributions to the student's process of *becoming*—it increases confidence and independence, strengthens the student's voice, and boosts sense of competence and maturity in the eyes of the parents. In addition, it deepens the sense of *belonging* for both students and parents. (See the book *Fostering Student Accountability through Student-Led Conferences* (Kinney, 2012) for more about this process.)

Top 8 Ways to Build Relationships with Parents

- Learn their names. Always greet them warmly whenever you see them, even briefly, and even outside of the school.

- Arrange to visit students' homes, particularly when students enter the middle grades.

- Have students take the lead at parent conferences.

- Invite parents to join the class for parties and presentations.

- Host a family cookout during school lunch time.

- Ask parents to write you a letter telling what is wonderful about their child.

- Frequently thank parents for their help and support. Do this privately and publicly.

- Treat parents as equals. Honor the parent-teacher partnership. Let them know you value them.

In their book *Reducing the Risk, Increasing the Promise* Sherrel Bergmann and Judith Allen Brough (2012) offer one clear caution about parent involvement: that teachers "don't give up on kids because of the actions or inactions of the parents!" (p. 113). We would add that teachers who value students' families also do not show favor to students whose parents **do** take an active part in supporting the teacher, class, or school. (For many more ideas to spark parent involvement, see *Teach My Kid I Dare You: The Educator's Essential Guide to Parent Involvement* (Bergmann, Brough, and Shepard, 2008).

For all that educators have learned in the past two decades about the value of building school communities, researchers still find a disparity between the understanding of the importance of school connectedness and the actual day-to-day practice of it. In *The Social Cure*, Jetten, Haslam, and Haslam (2011) refer to this as a persistent "blind spot" to the critical importance of satisfying social relationships. The value of social connection, they argue (and we heartily agree), cannot be underestimated.

Whether or not your school (or some of the folks in it) has any such blind spots, there are workable, effective steps you can take right away to move your school closer to a culture of connectedness that reaps benefits of increased *belonging* and *becoming* results for your students.

Putting It into Practice

As an individual, team, small group, or entire staff, use some of these activities to spark discussions, reflect on your current practices or situations, listen to others, or set goals.

1. Work alone, with your teammates, or with a few colleagues to answer this question: "How do students experience being members of this school (or my classroom)? How can I (we) tell?" Then identify practices that are already working to create a connected community in your classroom or school. Identify other practices or areas that you'd like to add or improve. Set time-frame goals for putting these to work.

2. Group discussion: What methods does your school have in place to ensure every student knows and has access to at least one adult on campus? Are the methods working for each student? If nothing is in place, what ways can you ensure each student is known and feels valued?

3. Hold a student focus group with students across all social groups; ask such questions as: "Do students in our school have a way to let adults know they have a need?" "If you or a friend had a problem, how likely would you be to seek help at school? Why or why not?" "Which adults would you or other students be most likely to approach?" "How can we do better at giving students a safe way to ask for help?"

4. Go to the website of the National Forum to Accelerate Middle-Grades Reform (www.middlegradesforum.org), and download the Schools to Watch Rubric. Individually complete the "Social Equity" section of the rubric. Tally the scores, and use the results as a springboard for a discussion on how your school meets the criteria.

Chapter 5

Believe in Students

"You can be the person who turns things around for students and liberates their learning paths. It usually takes just one person—a person whom students will never forget."

- Jo Boaler

When a person who accomplished something beyond what was expected, managed to graduate from high school or college against all odds from their life circumstances, or turned a trajectory of school failure into a successful path is asked, "What happened that enabled you to do this?"—how often does the response begin with, "There was this teacher . . ."?

Few educators get through teacher training without reading the landmark Rosenthal and Jacobson (1968) research study on how teacher expectations influence student performance. Researchers gave tests of intelligence and ability to students across six grades. They told teachers that, according to the test results, some of the students were capable of reaching their potential. Unknown to the teachers, the identified students were chosen at random. Their inclusion on the likely-to-succeed lists had nothing to do with abilities reflected on the tests. At the end of the year, researchers retested the students and found that those who had been identified to teachers as "ready to bloom" showed greater gains than those not identified.

The results of Rosenthal and Jacobson's experiments have been used to demonstrate the power of a "self-fulfilling prophecy" (also known as "the Pygmalion effect"): that students achieve the way teachers expect them to achieve (1968).

In a more recent study, teachers gave hundreds of adolescent students in their English classes helpful, specific feedback to written essays. On half of the papers, an extra sentence was added to the end of the feedback. The teachers did not know which students' papers had the sentence. (There were no other differences between the two groups of students.) Even a year later, students who received that sentence had higher grades in English classes. That one sentence was: "I am giving you this feedback because I believe in you" (Cohen & Garcia, 2014).

Such studies, along with the experiences of thousands of educators, show this: the beliefs that teachers hold about students (along with the words, nonverbal messages, and actions through which they communicate those beliefs) have powerful, long-lasting effects.

This may seem obvious—that we should believe in our students. But if any of us look closely, we'd likely have to admit that we **do** have preconceptions about students. Some students seem to constantly struggle, lag in engagement, or just be stuck in "not getting it." Others seem to be more motivated, work harder, and learn quickly. It's hard to look past the student behaviors, backgrounds, or attitudes and see students all as having equal chances of achieving. But because the messages we convey about individual students' possibilities for success make such a difference, we must pay close attention to our assumptions. Each adult in the school must do everything possible to show belief in every student.

Giving Students the Gift of Your Belief

Believing in every one of your students is one of the greatest gifts you can give. Let's take a look at what this means and why it matters. Believing in students means understanding that and acting as if every student has the capability to achieve and to grow in all aspects of *belonging* and *becoming*. The speed with which someone "gets" a concept, skill, or process is not indicative of her or his ability or potential. There are reasons for differences in performance (reasons that have nothing to do with inborn ability)—brains mature at different speeds; some students have had repeated failure experiences or negative messages; some may not have had nurturing, stimulating pre-school environments; some have lives outside school that inhibit their best performances; some have deep anxieties about social situations or peer relationships. When you believe in students, you don't equate performance with potential. Instead, you trust that the possibilities for high performance in academic and personal development are there for all students.

Take some time to go back and look at the lists you made for *belonging* and *becoming* as a task at the end of Chapter 1. (Or review Chapter 1.) Carefully look at every item on your lists or in the chapter in light of the concept of teacher belief in all students. Think about how letting students know you believe in them (or students feeling you don't believe in them) would affect each factor.

The strongest effect of believing in students is this: Your belief helps them believe in themselves. It increases their self-efficacy (belief that they are capable of achieving goals and meeting expectations). This mushrooms to such outcomes for students as the following (**all** of which build students' sense of *belonging* and skills and progress in *becoming*):

- Building intrinsic motivation.
- Understanding that, as individuals, they matter.
- Strengthening courage to take risks, to stretch beyond what they thought they could do.
- Boosting their confidence.

- Increasing the quality of the student-teacher relationship.
- Positively enhancing peer relationships.
- Helping them trust themselves more.
- Approaching challenging tasks with reduced anxiety.
- Decreasing anxieties about their abilities.
- Elevating empowerment—helping them feel more competent and independent.
- Igniting creativity.
- Increasing belief in (and thus, regard for) each other.
- Inspiring them to be persistent.
- Setting higher expectations for their next performance.
- Increasing resilience.
- Building passion, energy, and fun in learning.

Students' beliefs about themselves develop through their social interactions; and their social interactions with and assessments of peers mirror the teacher's beliefs and preferences (Osterman, 2000). So your belief in students spreads far beyond boosting their belief in themselves. It helps them see each other's worth and potential; they believe more in each other, and as they do so, the *belonging* and *becoming* benefits increase.

How do you let students know that you believe in them? Not just by telling them! Of course, encouraging words will be part of your ongoing messages to students. But your actions must **show** that you believe in them. All of us want to believe in students, and most of us feel we do

How do you let students know that you believe in them?

believe in students. But how often do we review last week's unit test and wonder in amazement at why so many students did poorly—and then place the blame on the students for their lack of preparation? Students have built-in fraud detectors. They will know if you're faking belief. (By the way, benefits of believing in students only result when you actually **do** believe.) You demonstrate that you believe in students when you

- Set high expectations and give clear guidance for how to meet them.
- Offer them lots of techniques and tools for succeeding at specific personal and academic tasks.
- Support, coach, and scaffold to help them succeed in academic and personal growth.
- Stay with them every step of the way as they tackle goals.
- Expect that they will achieve in different ways and on different timelines.
- Do not expect any students to fail. Help them recover when they do.
- Minimize competition among peers; help students see that they're competing with themselves.
- Encourage them not to put needless limitations on themselves (i.e., not to assume they can't do, learn, or change something).
- Give positive, specific feedback as encouragement, not as judgment.
- Let individuals know you believe they **can** do an assignment or pass a certain test.
- Give frequent messages to their parents that show you recognize their skills, efforts, talents, and progress—and that you believe they can achieve.
- Refuse to take part in conversations that complain about, label, or expect failure from individual students (yes, this means not whining about students in the teacher's lounge).
- Model persistence. Let them see you try something that is challenging for yourself. Let them teach you something (such as a new technical skill) and watch you push past your fears or awkwardness—working hard to master it. They can watch you believe in yourself!
- Encourage them to share goals and self-belief with one another and to support one another to believe in themselves. When a student sees someone else struggle and succeed, it increases the belief that she can do it herself. This is particularly true if that person has such similar characteristics as age, gender, ethnicity, or interests.

Making First Impressions

As students settle into their first class with you, let your belief in them be their first impression. During the opening day of school, start solidifying the message that this is a classroom and a school where each one of them can gain the skills of *belonging* and *becoming*. Let students know right away that this is a place with high expectations for knowledge and skills with many opportunities to grow academically and personally.

Reflect on your days as a student. Perhaps your typical first day of the school year was like this: Come in. Find your seat. Do not talk. Copy your schedule. Listen to the rules. Hear the consequences for breaking the rules. Read the syllabus (always scintillating reading). Fill out an information sheet with every piece of contact information short of giving a DNA sample. (After all, a teacher has to get that correct phone number before a misbehaving student does something wrong and then gives them a fake phone number!) Bell rings. Repeat the same cycle five or six more times that day.

Do you remember what your dinner table conversation was like the first day of school? Did anyone have anything exciting, fun, engaging, or positive to share about what happened? Or did you spend most of the evening hounding your parents to sign a bunch of paperwork that was due the next day to prevent you from having a lunch detention? If you are a parent now, is the cycle still the same (except that you are now the one being hounded to fill out all of that paperwork, read the parent-student handbook, and sign multiple pages of legalese you don't really read)?

Is the most important task in your school making sure that students know and follow the rules? If so, you will probably spend the first day talking to students about procedures, guidelines, rules, and consequences. This does not create a warm, inviting, or stimulating first impression. And it is definitely not an impression that shows students you believe in their capabilities to *become* or that leaves them feeling they truly *belong* in your classroom.

But if the most important aspects of your school and classroom are *belonging* and *becoming*, then break the pattern! Make your first impression as someone who is focused on believing that students can learn (this includes personal as well as academic learning) and assuring that you will help them all learn. Do not start your relationship with students by going over rules or procedures. Do not threaten consequences and punishment for failure to follow said rules and procedures. Let's face it—most students do the right thing most of the time. Let's treat them as if this is what we expect, rather than that we expect they might step out of line or fail at any minute.

In addition to setting a negative first impression, this focus-on-rules approach often backfires anyway. For the student who is prone to disregard guidelines, going over the rules (such as "Don't be tardy to class" or "Don't skip class") simply makes him think, "So, a bunch of people must be tardy or skip class, or she wouldn't be going over this in such detail. I'm glad it's not just me. I'll skip class when I feel like it."

For the student who has considered skipping class but hasn't for fear of possible consequences, giving the specific detailed consequences for each broken rule may make her think the consequences aren't really that bad. She might think, "Hey, it's only one day of in-school suspension for skipping class? Cool! I'm in!"

Then there's the student who would never dream of breaking the rules. He starts thinking back to the one time, last year, when he was late to class because he was sick in the bathroom. He worries about this all day, goes home and writes a letter of apology, and gives it to the teacher the next day. By going over rules and consequences, you've only made it more comfortable for misbehaving students to misbehave and more uncomfortable for students who are already doing the right thing. See Todd Whitaker's (2013) book *What Great Teachers Do Differently* for much more on this idea (pp. 13-18).

Instead of the usual going-over-the-rules-and-procedures approach, make the first day of school an "A" Day for you and your students. (We thank our colleague Bill Bond, former principal of Heath High School in Paducah, Kentucky for this idea.) Teach your most engaging, thought provoking, student-involved lesson of the year. Imagine a first day of school with 90 eighth graders outside learning about velocity by flying paper airplanes they just made in class, or getting first-hand experience of the concept of gravity when they float helium balloons, or understanding math by playing a game of cards with their friends (in groups), or dissecting a rat, or measuring shadows to learn the heights of the schoolyard trees, or exploring social studies concepts with a round-robin cooperative learning structure in a big circle outside on the grass (see Clowes, 2011, for an explanation of this learning structure).

In addition to getting them up, moving, and doing, make sure students leave that first class feeling believed in, trusted, and capable. Include strategies that invite them to work together, gain competence, use critical thinking skills, make independent or group decisions, create something, express their own opinions or reflections, receive positive feedback, and have fun. Now that is fodder for great dinner table conversations! "A" Day lets students see the very best you have to offer on the first day of school. It also lets them see the best **they** have to offer as students. You've let them know that you trust them to learn. You've let them know that they'll be learning from experiences that are lively and engaging and that this is what they can expect all year. Students will leave your class with a sense of anticipation; they'll be eager to return.

Solidifying First Impressions into Lasting Impressions

A middle school student in Texas described her early days of the school year this way: "Our teachers start out giving us trust, and it never goes away unless we break trust with them" (National Association of

Secondary School Principals, 2006, p. 68). How great to begin the school year with the model and promise of trust! Of course, this can't just be about the first day. The atmosphere, energy, dynamic learning, and belief you set on day one need to become the status quo for the whole year.

With a much more engaged audience after a great day of learning on day one, you can begin the business of collecting information and introducing guidelines on the days that follow. Involve students in decisions about classroom processes, guidelines for behavior, and consequences. Find ways for them to gain ownership in classroom procedures and expectations. Help them state guidelines in positive, rather than negative, terms. Regardless of when you choose to discuss codes of behavior, resist the urge to fall back into the "what-not-to-do" approach that leaves students feeling threatened, diminished, and untrusted.

> **The atmosphere, energy, dynamic learning, and belief you set on day one need to become the status quo for the whole year.**

Over the first week or two, gradually review the school-wide expectations that have been established. Teachers can do this in individual classrooms or host grade-level or team meetings. Approach this positively, sending the message to students that members of the school-wide community believe in them, expect the best of them, and don't anticipate bad decisions. Avoid emphasizing what happens when students make bad decisions. Student handbooks and word of mouth will take care of that! Here are some thoughts for a positive approach to the topic of school-wide guidelines:

Share the mission and commitment that is at the heart of the school. Sometimes the foundational beliefs, missions, and goals are shared only with adults. Students at this age are capable of interacting with this kind of information; they deserve to know what's behind the structure, programs, and practices of the school. Also give them a generic overview of teachers' preparation, degrees, and certifications. Introduce the concept of professional development—to let them know about the continued commitment to learning and improvement of skills and programs. (Some students don't realize that teachers actually have credentials to teach and also continue to "go to school" to learn more.)

Let students teach some of the specifics of school policies. For example, students can demonstrate the school dress code. Instead of you telling students what they can't wear, they can put together a fashion show to exhibit appropriate dress. (They love this, by the way.) They'll also enjoy bringing inappropriately dressed or misbehaving staff-member "models" before a panel of student "judges." They could even use the adult models for makeovers—showing them how to do a better job of dressing. (This works for other elements of the school codes as well.) Give a group of students responsibility for planning a grade level or school-wide assembly to share protocols and rules. They are much more creative than the adults, and the audience pays much closer attention when their peers are running the show.

Give credibility to school-wide procedures. Let students in on the "why" of school-wide practices. Explain the reasons for things such as the school's grading scale, mastery-based assessment model, final exam policy, cooperative discipline policy, required standardized assessments, or grade promotion requirements. This shows students you believe they are mature and smart enough to understand the need and reasons for a school-wide approach. These procedures become important parts of their learning, rather than things "done to them" that they don't have a clue what they are or why students have to follow them. When students see the purposes and realize that all teachers will consistently use these approaches, they may just tone down their complaints and give more support to their teachers who are implementing the requirements.

Emphasize the value of good decisions. Most schools have some sort of school-wide expectations (along with affirmations) for making wise choices. The bottom line is that we want students to make good decisions—not because they are afraid of getting in trouble if they don't and not because they want to please the adults—but because the decisions are healthy for the individuals and for the school community. Focus on the intrinsic rewards accompanying decisions that are helpful, respectful, safe, and growth-producing for self and others. It increases a student's sense of *belonging* to realize that her wise choices for herself benefit the others in her class and school. Expect the best of students. Expect good decisions, not foolish ones. Give lots of attention to the positive outcomes of "smart" decisions. If your school has a positive behavior support model, review the expectations (emphasis on what is expected, instead of what is not allowed). Then review how students will be supported and recognized for good decisions.

Recognize students' power in the school. Students may not see themselves as powerful in the school. Help them get a picture of the many ways they make a difference to the spirit, well-being, and success of others in the school community. Let them know how they can affirm others (including adults) and contribute to practices that help peers *belong* and meet their own goals (*become*). Review the ways they can develop and use leadership skills (see more on this in Chapter 8), *become* involved in school clubs, organizations, sports, arts, and activities; and take part in solving problems and making decisions that affect situations beyond themselves. Enthusiastically communicate the benefits of getting involved in school activities outside the classroom.

Share school-wide successes. We often share information about school-wide accomplishments with staff and parents, but students need this information, too. Describe the various school improvement efforts underway in the school. Tell them about results of school improvement efforts, and let them in on the future goals for improvement.

Share your school's successes in academics, athletics, activities, arts, and community service. Let students know how great their school is.

Promoting an Optimistic Outlook

Optimism—the tendency to look at favorable characteristics and possibilities and to expect the best possible outcome—is at the heart of believing in students. In an atmosphere of optimism, they'll be more likely to trust that you believe in them. In addition, their belief in themselves, belief in their peers, sense of *belonging*, and real hope for *becoming* what they want to be can **all** flourish.

Optimism is deeper and more active than just thinking positive thoughts or having generally good feelings about life. According to Martin Seligman (2006), a clinical researcher who has studied optimism and pessimism for decades, individuals have an "explanatory style"—a way they explain to themselves why things happen. According to his findings, optimists see causes of bad events as temporary and causes of good events as permanent. They can contain a bad event to a particular situation (seeing it as temporary) but believe good events to be broader. Optimists take credit for good outcomes and believe bad outcomes are caused by outside forces or chance and are not indications that they are undeserving or worthless.

Seligman also found that a child's explanatory style is learned—influenced by the style of his or her caretakers (they mimic those adults most prominent in their lives) and by the kind of criticism they get from those adults ("You'll never be able to learn this" vs. "You can get this if you practice more"). Both of these influences, certainly, have implications for teachers!

Optimism has been associated with several benefits—all of which we can recognize as characteristics we know can help satisfy our students' needs for *belonging* and *becoming*:

- Better relationships
- Less self-blaming, depression, and helplessness
- Less likelihood of giving up on challenges
- Greater ability to accept disappointments along with successes
- More hopefulness
- Increased confidence
- Better physical health
- Improved coping skills
- Greater persistence
- Increased productivity
- More feeling of control over one's life (Seligman, 2006; Sharot, 2011; Fox, 2012).

In our classrooms and the school community, we can promote optimism in many ways. All of the suggestions and strategies in the previous chapters and in chapters to follow contribute to an optimistic outlook. We can share our passion and enthusiasm for our jobs and for our students. We can help students let go of past failures and think about what they can do today and in the future. We can show them how to replace negative self-talk ("I can't," "This is too hard," "I give up," "I'm not good at this," or "I'll just mess up") with hopeful self-talk ("I couldn't last time, but maybe this time," "I'll give it another try," "I'll practice more," or "Maybe today this will work"). We can help students plan a course of action to tackle a challenge or problem and we can stick with them to help them stay focused on it. We can enlist our colleagues in consistently setting powerful examples of optimism in and outside the classroom. Most profoundly, we can **be** hopeful for each of them.

Top 8 Ways to Spread Optimism

- Begin the daily all-school announcements with an optimistic statement.

- Look for and reinforce examples of positivity, tenacity, and hope.

- Create a place and process for students to leave positive notes for each other.

- Ask students to brainstorm and practice ways to spread hope to one another.

- Celebrate persistence and hope as often as you celebrate proficiency.

- Expose students to models of adults and youth in society who display optimism.

- Invite students to suggest ways to turn pessimistic attitudes into optimistic attitudes.

- Refuse to repeat pessimistic statements or join in pessimistic conversations.

In the days after the Newtown tragedy, I (Laurie) wanted to share something with middle school teachers at our school that could be a small step toward building the kind of atmosphere that might prevent further tragedies. I showed a YouTube video, "Honk If You Love Someone," featuring a young man beside a street holding positive signs for people to see as they drove past. Some of the staff thought it was a bit "cheesy," and given our long-time open relationship, felt comfortable to tease me about it.

The following day, on my morning walk through the building, I heard a small commotion on a team hallway. Two of the teachers were holding up signs—clearly in an attempt to poke fun at my video idea. One read "SMILE," and the other read "IT'S A GREAT DAY TO BE A WILDCAT." But their plan for a funny response had an unexpected result. Their students got a kick out of the signs. The next day, the teachers held a new sign: "WE BELIEVE IN YOU!" Each day a new sign appeared. By the time state tests were given, the signs had daily themes. On the day of the science test, the sign read "MAY THE FORCE BE WITH YOU." On the day of the eighth grade dance, it was "DON'T JUST STAND THERE. BUST A MOVE."

What began as an inside joke became something that students anticipated. They had fun predicting what might be coming next. Simple signs such as "YOU'RE AMAZING" helped develop relationships and gave students an energizing, upbeat start to each day. Even the teachers were positively affected. One of the teachers who started it all said, "Quite simply, I think students feel we care about them. I can honestly say on a personal level that often their reactions are responsible for me having a better day."

Teachers also need support for being optimistic. For help recharging your own optimism, we highly recommend the book *Deliberate Optimism: Reclaiming the Joy in Education* (Silver, Berckemeyer, & Baenen, 2015).

Providing Instructional Support

When we hear a story about a teacher "who made a difference" in the life of a student, that story generally involves more than friendship or encouragement. In most cases, the teacher gave time and support that helped the student grow, stretch, reach, and achieve rigorous personal and academic goals. Models of effective schools that we've shared all include this component: they set high expectations and help students develop the self-belief, skills, and persistence to reach them. Research on developing caring, trusting relationships, showing belief in students, and building a connected community also include that same component as a factor. This is one of the strongest proofs that a teacher believes in a student: that the teacher (or whole "village") will help **students** to take charge of their own actions to bring about the results they want.

According to psychologist and self-efficacy researcher Albert Bandura (1995), the experience of mastery is the most critical influence on self-efficacy. Another strong influence is direct encouragement from a trusted person. A student concretely experiences a teacher's belief when that teacher gives specific techniques that enable the student to reach a goal.

Richard Curwin (2012), teacher, educational consultant, and author of *Discipline with Dignity*, suggests these ways to demonstrate your belief in students. We notice that they all relate to ways educators can adapt their instruction to enhance students' chances of achieving personal and academic goals. He says:

1) Stop using rewards.
   Extrinsic rewards are the opposite of believing they can do it without being "paid."

2) Encourage effort more than achievement.
   Doing one's best is one thing every student **can** do.

3) Give second, third, and fourth chances. Mistakes help people learn. Help student practice to learn the skills they need.

4) Don't say, "You failed"—say, "You haven't done it yet."
   Teach students that they **can** still do better.

5) Increase opportunities to learn.

The more chances students have to learn, the more they are likely to learn. Curwin notes that children who need extra and enriching learning opportunities are often the ones who lose them (because of things like behavior management or not finishing work).

Gone are the days when we focused simply on the quality of a teacher's presentations. The focus now is on students' learning. If a student is not learning, the finely honed craft of teaching hardly matters. We've enjoyed a cartoon that shows two boys standing near a dog while one boy tells the other, "I taught Hairy to whistle." The other boy replies that he doesn't hear Hairy whistling. The first boy responds, "I said I taught him. I didn't say he learned it!" How many times have we as teachers been guilty of believing we taught something, whether the students learned it or not?

Just as middle level students are at varying stages physically, the same is true for their cognitive development (which affects self-regulation as well as academic skills). Teachers must be willing to adapt instructional strategies to fit the individual student's cognitive development. Giving students the appropriate instructional support tells a student, "I believe in you." The way I taught the lesson the first time may not have worked for you, but that does not mean you cannot learn it. Let me try another way to help you understand." Teachers must become accomplished at scaffolding, teaming and co-teaching, using formative assessment to inform their instruction, designing cooperative learning experiences, re-teaching, adapting lessons to different modalities, incorporating technology, or doing whatever else it takes to help a student learn. One way, one time is no longer enough. As students see teachers make different and multiple attempts to help students learn, they will accept that the teacher believes in them. They'll begin to make progress and believe in themselves. (See more about instructional support in Chapter 6.)

Sadly, belief in oneself is often underrated in schools; at least, the nurturing of it is not a high priority. As we've come to understand that the mission of a middle school is entwined with helping students *belong* and *become*, we're more zealous about the importance of them believing in themselves. For once a student believes in herself or himself, possibilities for what she or he can be or *become* are limitless. In giving our students the gift of belief, we find Goethe's maxim to be a good reminder: "Treat people as if they were what they ought to be and you help them *become* what they are capable of *becoming*" (Litchfield Historical Society, 1968, p. 23). This isn't meant to sound easy. It's hard work—harder than many people outside the educational setting realize (think politicians). However, it is our mission. We're up to it!

Putting It into Practice

As an individual, team, small group, or entire staff, use some of these activities to spark discussions, reflect on your current practices or situations, listen to others, or set goals.

1. Ask each teacher to mentally review the first day of the school year, noting the activities and the amount of time spent on each task (i.e., rules? paperwork? class syllabus? instruction? active student participation?). Ask them to reflect upon the main purpose of the class and note the amount of the first day's time that was spent on that purpose. After completing this task, move to small groups and then to a large group to discuss the primary purpose of classes and how that purpose is reflected in your school.

2. Survey students. Find ways to get their (anonymous) feedback about the climate, community, and connectedness in the school. Take their feedback seriously. Use it to inform your next steps.

3. Have a small group of teachers walk through the school to look and listen for specific examples of how the school promotes an optimistic outlook for both students and teachers. Share the results with the staff as a whole. Then discuss strengths and needs for improvement in this area.

4. Examine how your school provides instructional support for struggling students. How many different instructional strategies do you use on a regular basis? What opportunities are there for professional learning to help teachers build repertoires of methods for helping struggling students? If the data are available, examine how many failing grades or less-than-proficient marks were given during the last grading period. Discuss strengths and needs for improvement in this area.

Chapter 6

Support Academic Success and Personal Development

> "Education, particularly in a democracy, has to involve heart as well as head, attitude as well as information, spirit as well as scholarship, and conscience as well as competence."
>
> - John H. Lounsbury

"Doing well in school" used to mean mastering content and skills—and getting good grades. In an age when we understand that we're teaching students, not just subject matter, we recognize that "doing well in school" is far more complex (and interesting)! Nowhere do *belonging* and *becoming* come together quite as powerfully for a young adolescent as when she or he steps into the world of academic learning. Our middle level students need to *belong* in order to *become* (in the sense of academic personal growth and accomplishment); in turn, their successes at *becoming* deepen the feelings and skills of *belonging*.

When we use the terms *academic success* and *personal development*, we're speaking of growth and learning comprised of the many aspects of both *belonging* and *becoming*. In a school setting, academic growth and personal growth are intricately intertwined with one another. It is nearly impossible (and not at all a good idea!) to talk about the details of one without including details of the other. Personal growth (in such areas as positive relationships, self-awareness, social awareness, self-regulation, decision-making, autonomy, personal responsibility, etc.) is absolutely needed for and contributes to the academic learning process. And when students experience what it feels like to take on an academic challenge and work hard to master it—skills of personal development get a boost.

Supporting young adolescents' academic and personal development jointly has **always** been a vital piece of the middle school concept. Back in 1963, William Alexander, one of the founders of the middle school movement, called for the development of schools for young adolescents that promoted academic achievement **by being more responsive to the personal needs of the age group** (Alexander, 2011). In the move to the middle school concept, schools put more focus on students' social and emotional development than had been the practice in junior high schools. As a result, middle level schools gained a reputation of being "soft" on academic rigor. The fact is that, from the beginning, the middle school concept has advocated for high expectations and academic growth—to be accomplished in a supportive environment that employs strategies appropriate for this age level.

> **Supporting young adolescents' academic and personal development jointly has always been a vital piece of the middle school concept.**

The concept sounds so obvious. Of course, we need to attend to the whole student. Of course, personal development is inseparable from academic growth. But doing it is not so simple, particularly at the middle level. Author and speaker Kari Kampakis (2015) notes, "It's rare to hear anyone say they loved middle school. Even people with positive memories don't tout the time as the best years of their lives. Simply put, it's an awkward season. It's a time of constant changes, social shake-ups, swinging emotions, and intense pressures" (para. 1-2).

The change and awkwardness of this "season" make it all the more critical that middle level educators understand the varied characteristics of the age group, the extreme differences in development, and the need and ways to teach personal and academic matters together. As teachers, we help students learn to break difficult tasks down into doable chunks. We want to follow this same tactic for our readers; so we'll suggest manageable ways to accomplish the long-term goal of nurturing academic achievement in combination with personal growth. In this chapter, we'll summarize what we find are best practices and attitudes to help students grow and thrive in the many aspects of *becoming* as related to their academic-personal development. In addition, we'll focus a bit more closely on practices that help you capitalize on students' strengths and interests, offer students opportunities to explore, contribute to the development of growth mindsets (in yourself and in students), help to cultivate students' resilience, and give students second (or more) chances to succeed.

Building and Bolstering the Underpinnings

Many elements of *becoming* fall into such categories as intrinsic motivation, engagement in learning, self-determination, self-efficacy, executive function and self-regulation, mindset, tenacity, personal responsibility, academic competence, and social and emotional competence. As is most likely true for you, we instinctively know that all of these are underpinnings of students' academic and personal growth. We've examined research, recalled our experiences, and listened to the experiences of many other educators—trying to understand what it is that helps students develop each of these elements in healthy, positive ways. We're astounded at the commonalities among the qualities, attitudes, and skills that constitute these elements—and at the practices that foster them (astounded, but not really surprised). We can't help but notice how often growth (or lack of growth) in each of these areas demonstrably affects the others. We can't help but notice how often *belonging* or *relatedness* is found by researchers to be a major influence on positive development in elements one might ordinarily put in a *becoming* category.

We believe that these commonalities lead to practical guidelines for schools and teachers to do two things: 1) celebrate and continue what they are already doing to enhance academic and personal growth, and 2) learn, incorporate, and polish what they could do better.

In an effort to reduce repetition that would result from addressing different aspects of academic or personal development, we'll share practices that, when combined, strengthen the underpinnings and desired outcomes of academic and personal education. Practices that we've described in the previous chapters (and in the chapters that follow) should certainly be added to these.

The Best Chances for Success

These are some of the most-often stated components or conditions found to increase young adolescent students' academic and personal development. Schools striving for the greatest possible effectiveness will do well to include them all in their vision and practice. Young adolescents are most likely to succeed in settings with

- High expectations, stated clearly.

- Support to reach the expectations.

- Equity in treatment of all students—along with equity in belief that all students are capable of learning.

- Emphasis on goals of learning over goals of grades or performance.

- Focus on students learning to set and attain goals.
- Highly effective, varied, and differentiated teaching and learning strategies.
- Teaching that is responsive to students' developmental characteristics and needs.
- Learning experiences that are relevant to students' interests and everyday lives.
- Learning experiences that engage students in active, participatory learning.
- Learning experiences that make use of student interests and strengths.
- Academic and personal challenge.
- Meaningful experiences of competence.
- Multiple opportunities for students to explore.
- Plenty of collaborative learning experiences.
- Precise, frequent, prompt, and supportive feedback.
- Opportunities for re-teaching and re-doing.
- Encouragement for student autonomy and empowerment.
- Trusting, caring, respectful relationships.
- Programs and practices that foster school relatedness and *belonging*.
- A sense of student ownership of the school, class, and their learning.
- Many opportunities for choice.
- Many opportunities for students to have a say in decisions and processes.
- Serious attention to social and emotional skills along with social and emotional supports.

Teaching Practices

The conditions that give our students the best chances for academic and personal growth lead to such practices as those that follow. Each of these practices includes skills and outcomes in many aspects of *belonging* and *becoming*.

Autonomy

Students feel more connected to learning when they have control over some of its elements. Autonomy is a major component of building competence, self-determination, self-efficacy, motivation, and engagement (Anderman & Patrick, 2012). Foster autonomy for young adolescent students in as many (appropriate) ways as possible. Give them plenty of chances to take initiative in classroom procedures and learning experiences. Ask them questions, and give them guidance that will help them solve problems on their own. Increase their chances for exercising choice and having a voice in their learning. Don't do for students what they can do for themselves. Show that you believe they can successfully exercise control over aspects of their learning. Supporting autonomy for students includes relinquishing some teacher control and using non-controlling language.

Relevance

Keep this on your radar screen at all times. Learning experiences should be meaningful—related to students' daily lives, to the important questions and concerns they have, and to the wider world in which they live. See that students understand why any particular assignment, activity, or fact is important—how it relates to the bigger picture. Always relate facts and ideas back to the main theme, concept, or skill being taught. Include topics and questions of their outside-school interests. Connect learning to pop culture, current events, situations in their school and community, current fads, popular music, social media, video games, relationships, and social and school issues. Use the technology and communications methods that are part of their young adolescent world as tools for learning. Part of the impetus for getting to know students as a group and individuals (Chapters 2 and 4) is so that you can relate their academic experiences to them personally. As a part of any learning experience, continuously ask students the questions "Why does this matter?" "So what?—what difference does this make?" and "How does this affect you?" Make a practice of having students stop at the end of a learning experience and write reflective paragraphs on how the skills or concepts relate to their lives.

Challenge

Humans learn best when they are challenged. Give students tasks and experiences slightly above their ability levels—so they need to stretch. Things that are too easy bore them. Things that are too hard frustrate them. (Provide the strategies, tools, and scaffolding to help them meet the challenge—if they need help.) Meeting slightly difficult challenges increases a student's sense of competence and self-belief. The more a student realizes "I can do this—even if it was a stretch!" the more the student will be willing to take on the next challenge.

Clear Expectations

It isn't fair to hold students to high expectations if they don't know what those expectations are. Be clear about what you're looking for—in terms of behavior, relationships, following procedures, and outcomes for any learning activity. Give students criteria for what mastery looks like. (Rubrics are one way to do this.) Share (in writing) the state standard(s) covered in a lesson or activity. State expectations in language students understand. Have them summarize, articulate, and discuss the expectations. They're more likely to meet expectations when there's no mystery about where they are going!

Instructional Support

Along with high expectations must come the instruction, support, encouragement, and time necessary for students to meet them. Excuses of "I have high expectations, but my students just don't meet them" are not allowed! Offer a range of paths and a variety of tools that can help them reach goals. Provide plenty of opportunities for them to succeed. Help students see what they already know about a topic or what skills they already have to follow a process. Differentiate assignments to accommodate needs of individual students. Scaffold tasks so that a student can meet a learning goal one step (or chunk) at a time. Encourage students to keep a journal of their accomplishments along the way. Be there to push them to do a little better than last time. But do not step in too quickly to rescue them; honor their autonomy and competence by letting them do it. When students stumble, help them see failure or road-blocks as things they can do something about.

Engaging Experiences

Here we might also use the term *active learning* or *student-centered learning*. Whatever you call the experiences, use learning strategies that get young adolescents involved physically, cognitively, behaviorally, and emotionally—**doing** instead of sitting and listening. With attention to their interests and their developmental needs (such as needs to find meaning, move, socialize, argue, or experience novelty), include such approaches as inquiry-based activities, interviews, demonstrations, cooperative learning, problem-solving, investigations, role-playing, brainstorming, peers teaching each other, frequent breaks to summarize or comment on what's been learned so far, debates, excursions, analyzing facts and concepts, or applying a process or concept to another situation. Include creative thinking, critical thinking, art, movement, media, technology, music (where possible), discussion, and humor. Have students draw on their previous learning and personal experiences to connect to the topic. And within all learning and curricular areas, students must have encouragement and specific experiences designed to let them explore, figure things out, exercise their creativity, and try new things.

Learning over Performance

When a student takes part in an activity with a goal of learning and understanding (this is referred to as a *mastery orientation*) instead of with the goal of getting a good grade, pleasing teachers or parents, looking smart, or doing better than other students (this is called a *performance orientation*), he or she is more likely to be deeply involved in the experience. The student is also more likely to want to follow through on the activity and achieve the goal. Students must experience mastery! Doing so heightens their feelings of competence (*becoming*), beliefs in themselves, and senses of *belonging*. Students with a performance orientation may avoid challenges, feel helpless when it gets hard, and give up easily—believing they don't have the ability to do the work. In contrast, when the goal is to learn, students are more likely to take on new challenges and are motivated to figure things out. You can encourage students' mastery orientations by reducing competition and comparisons between student accomplishments and by emphasizing individual progress and effort (and perhaps making sure grades and other assessments are private). When students meet a learning goal, provide lots of tools and ways to reflect on and demonstrate what they can **now do** or what they **now know**.

> **Students must experience mastery! Doing so heightens their feelings of competence (becoming), beliefs in themselves, and senses of belonging.**

Goal Setting and Attainment

Achievement, motivation, self-efficacy, and self-regulation increase when students set and pursue goals that are meaningful and appropriately challenging. Teach students strategies for setting and attaining goals. Then see that they have plenty of practice doing it. They need to learn to identify and set realistic, relevant, and rigorous goals. They need to be able to articulate their goals in specific terms and discuss how they will know when they reach them. Then give tools and training for each step toward goal attainment: making a realistic plan for reaching the goal, diagramming or otherwise outlining the plan, setting a timeline, breaking a long-term goal into short-term goals, and laying out specific approaches to accomplish for each part of the goal pursuit. Offer strategies for monitoring their progress and making needed adjustments in the plan if needed. Discuss what obstacles might interfere with their success and ideas for eliminating or circumventing the obstacles. Help them find ways to celebrate their goal attainment, too.

Collaborative Learning

Embrace collaborative learning as one of the most powerful forces for academic and personal development. Plan frequent partner and group experiences for making decisions, planning and carrying out projects, solving problems, carrying out investigations, asking and answering questions, and researching. In addition to being a boost to learning, understanding, and applying content, group work fosters student connections, communication, individual responsibility, group accountability, independence, and many skills of self-management. And it meets young adolescents' need for socialization. (The brain learns best in connection to other brains!) Take care to organize groups heterogeneously so students experience a mix of abilities, social groupings, genders, personalities, and ethnicities. In most cases, assign students to groups; when students choose groups, some students

> **Embrace collaborative learning as one of the most powerful forces for academic and personal development.**

feel left out and students don't get the benefits of true heterogeneous experiences.

Time

Students need time to absorb the meanings and implications of an activity. They need time to discuss concepts and see where they might lead. Too often we rush onto the next topic or activity. Plan ahead to include time for students to reflect, ask questions, voice opinions, hear ideas from others, write notes, and make connections.

Feedback

All students need (and deserve) feedback to get a sense of how they are doing in working toward a goal. Feedback of a timely and meaningful nature increases learning. The purpose of feedback is to strengthen skills or learn something. Avoid feedback that gives generalized praise ("Great job," "Nice work," or "A") or generalized criticism ("Try again," "Unclear," "Needs more development," or "C+"). Praise effort (with descriptions of specific actions) and progress toward goals—not ability or intelligence. Provide targeted, precise feedback that identifies how the student is doing in relationship to the goals and helps students know what action to take next. Feedback should be given soon after the task is completed (or during the process)—in time for the student to make changes while the material is fresh. Always give feedback in a positive spirit. Teach students how to give helpful, kind feedback to each other. Train students in ways to reflect on their work and design steps they can take based on their self-assessment.

Specific Skills to Teach

Students need planned, specific instruction dedicated to skills for "doing school." We've presented these in Figure 6-1 so you can identify those you already teach and those you wish to add to your classroom. Incorporate mini-lessons, roundtable discussions, video clips, or seminars to teach skills needed for learning in any subject area.

Figure 6-1   *Skills for Academic Success*

Already Do This (Date)	Will Add This (Date)	Specific Skills to Practice
		Participate in academic self-assessment and self-reflection.
		Take an active role in planning own learning.
		Set and attain goals.
		Give and receive feedback.
		Reason from credible evidence.
		Find and use strategies to solve problems.
		Make reasoned decisions.
		Explore; try new things.
		Manage time and assignments.
		Organize homework tasks.
		Transition between tasks.
		Get academic help when needed.
		Think about and describe thought or work processes (metacognition).
		Summarize.
		Report results.
		Ask good questions.
		Communicate effectively (in many different settings, situations, and formats).
		Listen actively and respectfully.
		Participate effectively in discussions.
		Work productively and cooperatively in groups.
		Keep up with a discussion or conversation.
		Take notes.
		Conduct an inquiry.
		Plan complicated projects.
		Complete complicated projects or abstract problems.
		Monitor and assess own progress (charts, checklists, journals).
		Learn from experiences.
		Learn from others who model skills.
		Bounce back from failure.
		Use mistakes as learning opportunities.
		Celebrate success.

Students also need direct instruction for skills of social and emotional health and behavior. This category of skills covers an extensive list of factors—all related to our goals of helping young adolescents in their processes of *belonging* and *becoming*. CASEL, the Collaborative for Academic, Social, and Emotional Learning (2017) has identified five broad social and emotional competencies with the following descriptions:

1) **Self-awareness:** The ability to accurately recognize one's own emotions, thoughts, and values and how they influence behavior. The ability to accurately assess one's strengths and limitations, with a well-grounded sense of confidence, optimism, and a "growth mindset."

2) **Self-management:** The ability to successfully regulate one's emotions, thoughts, and behaviors in different situations—effectively managing stress, controlling impulses, and motivating oneself. The ability to set and work toward personal and academic goals.

3) **Social awareness:** The ability to take the perspective of and empathize with others, including those from diverse backgrounds and cultures. The ability to understand social and ethical norms for behavior and recognize family, school, and community resources and supports.

4) **Relationship skills:** The ability to establish and maintain healthy and rewarding relationships with diverse individuals and groups. The ability to communicate clearly, listen well, cooperate with others, resist inappropriate social pressure, negotiate conflict constructively, and seek and offer help when needed.

5) **Responsible decision-making:** The ability to make constructive choices about personal behavior and social interactions based on ethical standards, safety concerns, and social norms. The realistic evaluation of consequences of various actions and a consideration of the well-being of oneself and others.

From this description of social and emotional competencies, teachers can extrapolate lessons to be taught and skills to be reinforced. We would suggest that you teach mini-lessons involving role-play, group discussion, brainstorming, and lots of student input and experience-sharing to teach and practice skills such as those on Figure 6-2.

Figure 6-2 *Social-Emotional Skills*

Already Do This (Date)	Will Add This (Date)	Specific Skills to Practice
		Recognize and celebrate one's own strengths and talents.
		Identify one's own challenges.
		Identify one's own needs, interests, goals, dreams, preferences, values, hopes.
		Identify emotions.
		Identify things that trigger different emotions.
		Build self-confidence.
		Set and attain personal (non-academic) goals.
		Appreciate diversity.
		Empathize with others.
		Treat others respectfully.
		Build and sustain relationships.
		Work with a team.
		Take responsibility for one's own actions.
		Examine one's own motivations.
		Understand motivations of others.
		Identify stressors, symptoms of stress, and ways to manage normal daily stress.
		Learn and use emotional coping skills (in response to disappointment, confusion, worry, fear, anger, insecurity, powerlessness, frustration, anxiety).
		Persevere.
		Bounce back from disappointment or failure.
		Identify and describe personal or social problems.
		Analyze situations.
		Identify and solve problems.
		Get help for problems or issues.
		Deal with social issues.
		Advocate for one's self.
		Deal with change.
		Screen out distractions.

See the new, dynamite resources for teaching social-emotional skills by Debbie Silver and Dedra Stafford (2017): *Teaching Kids to Thrive* and the Thrive website www.teachingkidstothrive.com.

And before we leave the topic of practices and skills that build and strengthen the underpinnings of academic success and personal development, let us not forget who it is that daily, consistently demonstrates to students how to do these things we want them to learn and develop. Yes, their peers are strong influences. But at the middle level ages, adults (particularly trusted adults) still influence them most. Students are watching all your academic, ethical, social, and emotional behaviors. Model the attitudes, values, behaviors, passions, reactions, mindsets, and relationships that you hope students will develop.

Capitalizing on Students' Strengths and Interests

Anthony is passionate about robotics. Right now, in his seventh-grade social studies class, he's deep into researching to create a visual presentation that includes a history of robotics along with a step-by-step lesson on how to make your own simple robot. Up until now, Anthony has been enthralled with the building process. But now, he's also awed by what he's learned beyond the actual mechanics.

Natalia has become quite good at writing and performing rap music. She's using her sixth-grade language arts writing project as a way to teach others about the structure, themes, influences, and history of rap music. She plans to involve the class by pairing up other students and guiding them in a rap-writing session. She says her "mind is blown" by what she's learned about the beginnings, development, and impact of rap.

A century ago, John Dewey said, "Persons, children or adults, are interested in what they can do successfully, in what they approach with confidence and engage in with a sense of accomplishment" (p. 1, 1913). What better way is there to engage a student in meaningful, challenging learning than to start with a skill she already has or a pursuit that has already grabbed his interest? When you start with what students **already know or can do**, they have the advantage of beginning from a place of comfort—from a place where they already have some success. You can help them build from there, adding challenge, sending them in new directions to deepen understanding, to add more knowledge, to dig into aspects of their interests that they never thought to explore, to apply the knowledge or skills in new places, and even to teach what they know to other students.

Students must consider a learning experience personally meaningful and relevant—worthy of their time and effort. They must be able to connect it to their experiences, their lives outside of school, the world they know, and things they know. When learning is built around student interests, areas of curiosity, areas of strength and confidence, or special areas of their knowledge or accomplishment, they do better in school. They are more motivated, pay attention more closely, and care more about understanding the material. They are more likely to apply new concepts to their lives, to work harder, and to persist longer (Bell, 2010; Dewey, 1913; Jensen, 2008; Martin & Dowson, 2009; Sternberg, 2000; Sternberg & Grigoranko, 2000).

We know that many student interests are fluid; young adolescents often hop from one passion to another. They try one sport after another, one club after another, or one instrument after another. Well, that is normal. Frustrating as it may be for adults, this is just what we know is good for them—to explore many activities, skills, and interests. With each new interest or skill, there are more topics with which to engage them. But not all of their interests are fleeting. As Dr. Mel Levine (2012) pointed out in an interview on the topic of student strengths and affinities, specific personal talents and interests are what lead many people to success in school or life. He added that some of the things that can cause a kid a lot of trouble in fourth grade can turn out to be the reasons she or he *becomes* a CEO later on (Scherer, 2006).

To connect learning to students' interests and strengths means, of course, that we must know what those interests and strengths are.

This is why teachers work at thoroughly understanding the characteristics of young adolescents. This explains the emphasis on getting to know students as individuals and keeping that going all year long. (Remember Chapter 2?) All that information you collected about students and the strategies you've learned for keeping up on their interests is a valuable base for making learning relevant to their lives and talents.

Capitalizing on students' interests and strengths also means continuing to notice (or finding out) what interests them and what strengths they're developing. Pay attention to their favorite fads, music, videos, out-of-school and in-school activities, social concerns, questions about the world, problems, dilemmas, current events that affect them, hopes, and dreams. Notice what ignites or worries them. Embrace the technology that is such a huge part of their lives, understanding that just about all of them are skilled with this. They already are global networkers!

There are many ways to honor students' interests and strengths and many ways to make use of these to enhance their learning. This can take the form of individual students' learning pursuits or lesson adaptations that teach to the interests of the whole group. The commitment to this should pervade all decisions about what and how to teach. When we see that young adolescents have a significant say and plenty of choice in their learning, we capitalize on both their interests and strengths. (See practices for this in Chapter 7.) When we know students love to explore—particularly outside—and we turn our Lewis and Clark history lesson into an outdoor expedition with canteens of water and tattered maps of clues for them to follow, we capitalize on their interests. When we pay attention to their love for socializing and adapt our choral music practice schedule to allow some time for this, we honor their interests. When we notice their increasing skills of autonomy and thus turn over planning of the next math unit to the students, we capitalize on their strengths. Our efforts to mix learning with their strengths and interests yields benefits beyond increased academic learning: deeper teacher-student relationships, clear demonstrations to students that we believe in them, greater self-efficacy for students, and increased experiences of *belonging*.

On the other hand, when students socialize too much or too vigorously and we institute a silent lunch or shorten their break times, we ignore the benefits that come from embracing students' interests. (By the way, social skills they practice at school are critical aspects of *becoming* and *belonging*.) Whenever we disregard, minimize, or, worse, take away what students value—what they spend the rest of their lives doing (when not in class), we set up a situation of *us* versus *them*, of it being *our* school instead of *their* school.

Unfortunately, we see many practices that limit some middle level students' access to or participation in the very learning experiences that engage them most. The United States' (almost exclusive) emphasis on reading and math has led to situations where schools heavily focus teaching time on what will be "on the test." This approach decreases time and opportunities for students to explore, for teachers to plan lessons around students' interests and strengths, and for students to thrive in other subjects. Such practices affect all students; but it seems that struggling students are most affected. We must find a way to preteach and reteach difficult math concepts without removing a student from his favorite vocational arts class or from her graphic design exploratory hour in order to do so. We must find ways to close students' academic gaps without offering a make-up reading class during the one class period when the student can take band.

Our friend and colleague Dr. Betty Crocker shared an experience about her middle school's proposed plan to replace science class for below-grade-level readers with extra reading instruction. On pages 235–236 in this book (Appendix C), see her account of how she responded to this by changing her science instruction in a way that addressed the reading problems while keeping students in the science class they loved.

We see similar examples with students' participation in athletics, other extra-curricular activities, and exploratory classes. Most often, when a student is not performing well in class, it is due to a skills gap, a disability, a difficult home life, or poor work ethic. We tend to be a little more understanding of the first three and get really frustrated with the fourth. There are plenty of times when a student with a poor work ethic is still able to survive academically while the hard-working student putting forth strong effort simply cannot master the required standards. Which of these students is more likely to be restricted from participating in extra-curricular activities or exploratory classes that allow her to use her greatest strengths or follow her greatest interests? The one who cannot "make the grade."

"No research supports the idea that low grades prompt students to try harder. More often, low grades prompt students to withdraw from learning" (Guskey, 2011, p. 21). In order to capitalize on students' strengths and enhance their learning by involving them with what they value, schools must find ways to avoid punishing students for skills gaps while they reward students who do not have these gaps. Allowing a student's skills gap, disability, or difficult home life to determine his eligibility to participate in exploratory classes, athletics, clubs, musical groups, or other extra-curricular activities deprives him of some of the most meaningful, engaging learning experiences the school can offer to him.

Offering Students Opportunities to Explore

The middle school is the finding place; for young adolescents, by nature, are adventuresome, curious explorers. Therefore, the general approach for the entire curriculum at this level should be exploratory. Exploration, in fact, is the aspect of a successful middle school curriculum that most directly and fully reflects the nature and needs of the majority of young adolescents, most of whom are ready for an exploratory process. Although some experiences may be labeled exploratory, it should not be assumed that they are, therefore, nonacademic. The reverse is equally true; a solid academic experience properly designed is exploratory. Exploration is an attitude and approach, not a classification of content (National Middle School Association, 2010, p. 20).

By the time they reach middle school, some students are developing into debaters, animators, dancers, volleyball stars, trumpet players, graphic artists, mechanics, cooks, writers, photographers, forensic scientists, fashion designers, naturalists, tech wizards, coding experts . . . and more! Some have been specializing since their parents signed them up for Lego club or soccer when they were three years old. Others haven't had enough opportunities during or outside of school to know what they like and want to be able to do. For both of these groups, and for those in between, middle school is a time to explore, to take on a new hobby or skill, broaden their views of themselves, learn about capabilities they didn't know they had, be exposed to possibilities they'd not previously considered—or possibilities they never dreamed they could touch.

Young adolescents should have chances to explore everything (well, almost everything)! As we said earlier, exploration should be a part of many learning experiences in every classroom and in every part of the curriculum. In addition, a school's elective or exploratory classes offer great avenues for a student to explore new possibilities or deepen skills and knowledge about an interest he already has. There are dozens of topics and skills for exploratory classes at the middle level and numerous structures and schedules by which they can be included in the curriculum.

In the "middle"—between elementary and high school, we must balance opportunities for students so that there are both required courses (for exposure) and choice courses (for honoring what students value and developing new interests). This structured choice can lead a student who would never choose to pursue art on her own to begin to develop her talent after taking an art course, while allowing the already budding artist to further develop his talents. Many middle schools require some exploratory courses (such as technology) while allowing students to choose from a selection of other courses. Others offer a rotation of required "elective" classes for the younger grade levels, giving students more choices as they progress through the grades. For times when a formal course cannot be offered due to scheduling conflicts or available resources, informal mini-classes, clubs, independent studies for individuals taught by "expert" volunteers, after-school programs, or participation in community programs can also help students find places to *belong* and develop skills for *becoming* something new.

Some Topics for Exploration

animation	engineering	graphic design	researching
archaeology	entrepreneurship	journalism	robotics
architecture	ethnic studies	languages	rocketry
astronomy	film making	mechanics	song writing
broadcasting	first aid	medicine	stock market
business skills	forensic science	performing arts	rocketry
choral music	food science	personal finance	theater
coding	gaming	photography	web design
creative writing	geology	pop culture	woodworking
dancing	creating apps	problem solving	video making
debate	fashion design	psychology	video game development
digital presentations	global issues		

Developing a Growth Mindset

Often a student says, "I can't do that." And too often, a teacher thinks about a student, "She can't do that." Every student needs a mentality shift that allows her to say, instead, "I can't do that **yet**." And every student deserves teachers with the same mentality shift—teachers who think, "She can't do that **yet**."

Stanford psychologist Carol Dweck (2007) spent three decades researching why some students achieve their potential while others with just as much intellectual ability do not. She concluded that students' motivation and achievement were affected by their mindsets—their underlying beliefs about whether their abilities were fixed at birth or could be developed.

Dweck shared the discoveries and insights of her research in her book *Mindset: The New Psychology of Success* (2007). She coined the term *growth mindset* to describe the belief that intelligence and abilities (including their own) can improve and develop over time and the term *fixed mindset* to describe the often-held belief that people (including themselves) are simply born with certain intelligence and abilities that they can't do much to change. Furthermore—and very exciting— Dweck found that mindset could be changed through specific teaching and learning efforts and that changing to a growth mindset could significantly boost students' achievement. Her research also found that teachers' mindsets affect the beliefs that students have about their abilities and thus their mindsets (2007, 2015).

In the last decade or so, understandings about mindsets have made a major impact on education. Thousands of educators have applied the principles to promote dramatic changes for students. When students believe that their current performances can be improved, they take on a mindset that says "While I can't do it right now, with hard work, I can improve." With this belief, they are more motivated to work toward growth and improvement. And, when teachers have the same growth mindset—believing that students can improve through hard work and perseverance, they are likely to expect more from their students. Instead of thinking, "This student can't do this" or "This student is doing the best she can do," the teacher thinks, "There are many possibilities for what this student can learn; let's see what they are!"

A body of research shows that a growth mindset can improve performance and help students retain learning long-term (Dweck, 2007). A growth mindset supports self-efficacy—a person's belief in his ability to succeed or accomplish a task (Dweck, 2007). Not only can we encourage students to believe in themselves and their abilities to take on challenging tasks—we can share what's been learned about the brain! We can teach students that it is possible to "grow their brains" and achieve more (Dweck, 2015). In tandem with self-efficacy, a growth mindset contributes in dynamic ways to a young adolescent's *becoming* successful now and in the future. "Smart is not something you just are; smart is

"Smart is not something you just are; smart is something you can get."

something you can **get**" (Efficacy Institute, 2008, p. 1)! (As an interesting aside, Dr. Carol Dweck took up piano as an adult and learned to speak Italian in her 50s [Krakovsky, 2007]).

Many years before the concept of mindsets was a hot topic in education and the term *growth mindset* was in vogue, I (Patti) learned an important lesson from one of my sixth-grade students. Mark was a bright kid who was on an IEP, having been diagnosed with a learning disability in reading that had caused him to be reading several years below grade level. Whenever a task involved a considerable amount of reading, Mark would become frustrated, upset with his inability to read and comprehend as easily as other students. Often, he dissolved into tears and usually just gave up. When I talked with him about this, it was clear that he thought of himself as "dumb," regardless of the fact that he was doing fairly well in other subjects, especially in ecological science—an area of special interest to him.

Despite numerous discussions, nothing seemed to convince him that he wasn't "dumb." One day I tried a slightly different approach based on something I had read about brain research. I explained to him that it wasn't that he was dumb; it was just that his brain was wired differently from many other students and so it took a longer time for him to understand what he was reading. I told him that, for example, many brains translated reading by going from point A to point B to point C and so forth. His brain might need to process the ideas by going from point A to point C back to point A, jump ahead to point D and then return to point B. (Please remember this was back in the 80s, not as much was known about how the brain operated, and the explanation was not based on deep brain research but was rather a desperate teacher trying to help a student understand why he wasn't reading as well other students his age and that it was important to keep trying!)

It's likely that Mark had heard other explanations of why he struggled in reading. But for some reason, at this particular point, this explanation clicked with him. He seemed to take it as an assurance that maybe, if he kept at it, he would get better at reading. When I saw how Mark responded to this new understanding about his brain, I was inspired to try some new strategies. I started by helping him set short-term, reachable reading goals. Then I paired him with another student and showed them a tactic called "say something" for increasing comprehension. They stopped at the end of each short section and said something— asking a question about the text, connecting something from the text to a personal experience, making a prediction about what might come next, or making an inference about what something meant.

Mark started to put more effort into trying to read, and his ability to read did improve. It didn't happen overnight or without struggles. But shifting his thinking from "I'm dumb and can't read" to "Maybe I can learn to read better if I try harder" made a difference. And by the way, today he is a contributing member of his community and owns his own business (and yes, it has to do with the outdoors—his middle grades interest).

Now I understand that I had helped Mark begin to develop a growth mindset. In addition, I had instinctively tried some different strategies to support the spark of understanding about his brain.

I (Laurie) also learned something several years ago that I now realize had to do with fixed mindsets (though I didn't use that terminology at the time) and the ability to change them. I remember a student, Kyle, in the middle school where I was principal. Like the boy in Patti's story, Kyle had an IEP based on his documented disability. Unlike Mark, Kyle struggled in all of his classes. Also unlike Mark, Kyle had a pretty upbeat attitude about his classes and didn't seem to let the challenges he faced get him down. His teachers, however, were not as confident in Kyle's ability to make progress toward his learning goals. In addition to overcoming the barrier of concerns they had about his ability to learn, they had to grapple with questions about their own skills to help him. They were stuck in a place of little hope for him and for themselves.

But together Kyle's teachers gathered the courage to face their insecurities and try something different. Teachers who were using a co-teaching model began by welcoming Kyle into their general education classrooms. With the assistance of Kyle's paraprofessional, they were able to make specific plans for Kyle's daily instruction (differentiation at its best) while still attending to the needs of other students. In addition, they moved away from judging Kyle's success only on his proficiency with the content standards. They began to look at his growth as the greatest measure of his success. Though he did not always show proficiency on standards, he did meet his own growth goals. This gave a boost to everyone involved. Kyle's teachers adopted the motto "fair does not mean equal." It took time, collaboration, risks (and failures), lots of differentiation, and patience—but their beliefs about Kyle's abilities changed. And instead of seeing (and worrying about) what Kyle **couldn't** do, they looked for and found what Kyle **could** do.

One of the things we both learned from these students and see more clearly now that we know about mindsets is that a growth mindset is not just about a student or teacher trying harder. In her 2015 article, *"Carol Dweck Revisits the 'Growth Mindset',"* Dr. Dweck says,

> . . . a growth mindset isn't just about effort. Certainly effort is key for students' achievement, but it's not the only thing. Students need to try new strategies and seek input from others when they're stuck. They need a repertoire of approaches—not just sheer effort—to learn and improve (p. 20).

Dweck is speaking here about students, but the same holds true for teachers and all other persons who move toward a growth mindset. In one of the stories told from our past, Mark not only tried harder but also took advantage of some specific strategies offered by the teacher and assisted by a peer. In the other story, the teachers put forth more effort for Kyle. But that was not all they did; they also took different actions. They took a risk, stepped out of their comfort zones, and changed the way they operated.

The Teacher's Mindset

While the education world is abuzz with ways to help students develop growth mindsets, we often forget about the teacher's mindset. As is true with the teacher's self-efficacy and belief in students, the teacher's mindset influences his or her students' mindsets. When a teacher has a growth mindset, students are more likely to change mindsets and believe they can learn if they work hard and use specific strategies and assistance from others. But this has to be a genuine mindset, not just lip service to the concept. Many teachers say they have a growth mindset, but their classroom behaviors and practices don't match their statements. Students sense the teacher's beliefs. They know when a teacher has his mind made up about a student's abilities. It is very difficult to help a student feel as though she *belongs* in a class and that she can *become* (meet goals of the class) when she senses that the teacher has doubts—for whatever reasons—that she belongs there or can reach the goals.

Researchers Rattan, Good, and Dweck (2012) suggest that when students are struggling, teachers show a growth mindset not by comforting the students ("Oh, I see you're having a hard time with this. Lots of students struggle with writing") but by giving them specific strategies they can use to make progress. Middle level expert and author Debbie Silver (2012) explained it this way: "Rather than just admonishing students to work hard at something, we need to model the effective preparation we want them to use. Whether we are talking about a study skill, an athletic performance, or some other area, we need to guide students in specific techniques for practicing effectively and efficiently" (pp. 92-93). In other words, "just try harder" doesn't cut it!

Here are some ways teachers can work toward having a growth mindset more often and about more students.

Reflect on your own mindset. Pay attention to beliefs you have about students—to your thoughts, explanations, and statements. Notice if you place blame when frustrated and where you place it. Do you hear yourself saying such things as these?

"I have high expectations. Students just aren't meeting them."

"I've taught the material, but students just didn't pay attention."

"I've reviewed this a thousand times; students need to do their homework."

"These students are doing the best they can considering their lives at home; they can't do any better than this."

Think of yourself as a learner. You are capable of getting smarter, too! Do you believe that you have capabilities to learn new things, teach better, develop your brain, succeed with new programs and strategies? (You can!)

Learn from your peers. One of the best ways to learn a growth mindset is to watch it at work in others—particularly people close to you, people who have similar jobs and challenges as you, and people you admire. In turn, try to model growth mindset for others.

Support professional development in growth mindset. Everyone in a middle school will benefit from increases in growth mindset. Encourage your school to dedicate time and resources to providing training for staff (all staff) in this quality. Just as we need to help students with specific practices to change their mindsets and make academic and personal progress, so teachers need concrete actions to have growth mindsets more often. Remember, it doesn't come just from trying harder!

Support each other. Ask for and give feedback to colleagues. Commit to reflecting on your own mindset and the manifestations of each other's. Commit to helping each other grow.

Don't expect perfection. Don't assume that you or anyone else has or will have a 100% growth mindset. In an interview with Christine Gross-Loh of *The Atlantic*, Carol Dweck said that "nobody has a growth mindset in everything all the time" (para. 11). Working toward a growth mindset is a lifelong process. As with many other positive and healthy behaviors, keep practicing it in all areas of your life.

Students' Mindsets

The good news about mindsets is that they **can** change. Help students believe that ability is not fixed but that it can grow. Make sure each student understands that this means him or her and all the other kids in the school. Think of what this can do for students' senses of *belonging*—to know that the other students believe he or she **can** do better! See the following practices to help students develop or increase growth mindsets. We guarantee that some of these will sound familiar; they're the same practices that affect so many other facets of academic and personal growth (of *belonging* and *becoming*).

- Consistently reflect on your own mindset.

- Model a growth mindset.

- Build camaraderie with students in the pursuit of a growth mindset; let them know that most people question their own capabilities or fear they can't do better at something (this includes you).

- Focus on learning rather than performance.

- Give students opportunities to redo and fix their work.

- Encourage students to seek and tackle challenges.

- Praise students for effort, persistence, working toward a goal, taking on a challenge—but not for ability.

- Give feedback that is specific and leaves the student knowing what to do next.

- Foster autonomy; let students have control over some of their own learning.

- Give students time and ways to examine and explain their mistakes.

- Watch how you react to mistakes. (Do you see them as "bad" or harmful?)

- Always show students how they can learn from correcting mistakes (not from **making** mistakes—but from **correcting** mistakes).

- When students struggle, don't assign this to their intelligence (or ability).

- Teach students that struggling is not a bad thing; instead it means you're working hard at something that is important!

- Teach students about neuroplasticity—about how brains can change and grow smarter.

- Shore up positive classroom relationships, students' self-efficacy, and students' senses of *belonging*.

- Design the kinds of learning experiences students deserve—relevant, honoring their interests and talents, and full of action, collaboration, and engagement.

- Teach growth mindset hand in hand with study skills, skills of self-regulation, specific skills of content areas, and other specific academic and personal skills. (See skills listed on pages 102 and 104.)

When answering questions about what teachers can do to foster growth mindsets for students, Carol Dweck said, "Focus on the learning process and show how hard work, good strategies, and good use of resources lead to better learning" (Gross-Loh, 2016).

Cultivating Resilience

Resilience is the ability to recover from difficulties, serious hardship, or adversity—all the attributes, attitudes, resources, and skills a person has to cope and take care of himself or herself in hard times. There are times in some lives when resilience must be defined as the capacity and capability (through a set of skills) to adapt to circumstances that threaten their very lives, development, or function—and to adapt in ways that lead to positive functioning. Harvard Medical School psychologist Dr. Robert Brooks (2013) has studied resilience for decades. He is the author of many books on resilience, including *Raising Resilient Children* (Brooks & Goldstein, 2002). In response to a question about his definition of resilience, he explained:

> The main way I look at resilience is the capacity for people who have faced adversity to bounce back and to cope much more effectively with life. I see it as people who really have very good coping strategies. And they also have an optimistic attitude. They feel that even though they have faced difficult times, that there are ways they can overcome them (0:15-0:39).

All of us experience adversity. It's a part of human life. It's inevitable that our students will encounter stress, disappointment, failure, illnesses, accidents, and setbacks. Some of this happens in school. Much of it comes from their lives outside school. Some of our students experience acute stress, chronic difficulties, terrible tragedies, or trauma.

Whatever adversity they meet, they come into our classrooms and our care, and we must do everything possible to help them recover and go on with life to experience hope and joy.

We would love to keep our students and our own children from having setbacks, devastating changes, and probably all adversities. We can't do that. But the good news is that resilience can be developed. According to Dr. Brooks (2015), his research on resilience has consistently shown one essential factor in helping children cope with adversity and *become* resilient. That is having at least one of what he calls "a charismatic adult" in the child's life—"an adult from whom a child gathers strength." He goes on to say, "So the person feels that, okay, I'm having some difficult times but there can be better times ahead. Also what the charismatic adult does is help the person see that they have the resources within themselves to start to make these changes" (2012, 0:53-1:22).

As teachers, we can each be an adult from whom our students gather strength. We can model resilience, but we can't do it for them. We **can** be there for them. We **can** communicate unconditional acceptance. We **can** help them gain the attributes that enable them to find the resources within themselves to increase resilience. And we **can** help students develop a resilient mindset—a "relative" of a growth mindset. If a person

> As teachers, we can each be an adult from whom our students gather strength.

of any age or situation is to bounce back from difficulty, he or she must believe that it's possible to do better, to get better, to survive and thrive. With a growth mindset, a student believes that his or her brain can develop to learn and accomplish things. With a resilient mindset, the student believes that there are things he or she can do to recover from hardship and to thrive.

A working paper from the Center on the Developing Child at Harvard University (2015) summarized the other conditions that counterbalance the negative effects of significant adversity for children (conditions other than having the significant adult relationship). These are all conditions that involve one or more adults in an assisting role:

- Help to identify their strengths (often called "islands of competence") and build belief in their personal control—belief that they have the resources to solve problems and influence what happens in their lives.
- Help learning and practicing skills for adapting to the difficult situation—skills of self-regulation, decision-making, planning, coping, and controlling emotions.
- Help and encouragement in finding ways to enrich the lives of others.

A guidebook on resilience from the Parenting for Life program, sponsored by the Psychology Foundation of Canada (Hoffman, 2017), adds these conditions:

- A sense of *belonging* and knowing how to reach out to people who are there for them.
- Developing optimism and hope.

We want our students to thrive. Encouraging persistence, grit, and resilience takes a set of skills that is sometimes overlooked. Students need to learn how to deal with struggle—believing in themselves, managing their emotions, and finding healthy responses. As educators, we are right there in position to help students learn tools to help themselves overcome stress, mistakes, failures, unexpected changes, setbacks, and other adversities without sinking into depression or hopelessness, giving up, or blaming their struggles on what they think is their own innate ability to make things better. We (the authors) are not big fans of the catchphrase "Failure is not an option." Failure (like disappointment and many other adversities) is always an option—an expected part of life. We would rather students see that giving up is not an option.

Top 13 Ways to Cultivate Resilience

- Model resilience and optimism.

- Let students gather strength from you.

- Help them express their emotions.

- Show them how to turn negative thoughts and statements into positive ones.

- Encourage appropriate assertiveness.

- Help them belong in the school setting.

- Help them identify their own inner resources they can use to overcome their problems.

- Increase their self-belief.

- Boost their sense of autonomy and competence.

- Share real-life and literary examples of people who recovered from adversities.

- Remind them that you believe in them.

- Teach them coping skills.

- Help them find ways to help others.

During this quickly changing time of a young adolescent's development, students are developing habits and traits that they will carry into adulthood. Although it is never too late to develop resilience, it is far easier for young people to learn now rather than later to accept and cope with adversity. And developing the skills and mindset of resilience gives them much greater chances for having fulfilling, balanced lives. It's heartening to know that teachers and schools have a key role in building resilience—and that what we do can make substantial differences for our students. "Experts have different theories and terms for talking about resiliency, but one point is unanimous among them: *the single most important factor in child resiliency is relationships*" (Hoffman, 2017, p. 4).

Giving Second (and Third and Fourth) Chances

If we believe that challenge, self-belief, mastery, goal attainment, autonomy, learning from correcting one's mistakes, competence-building, perseverance, resilience, and growth mindset contribute to academic success and personal development, then why would we give students just one chance to reach such a goal as completing a project, doing well on an assignment, writing a paper, or passing a test? How dare we say, "You can't keep trying," "You can't show that you can do better," or "Sorry, even if you worked hard, that was your only chance to get this right"!

Many students need more than one chance to learn a concept and demonstrate knowledge of that concept. In the same light, some students need far more than basic content knowledge and must be given opportunities to go beyond the basic requirements of school. No two students are alike, but all students deserve "whatever it takes" to help them *become* the most successful students possible. Thus, it is a teacher's responsibility to do everything possible to ensure all students meet not only the required learning goals but also the goals appropriate for each student. Just as we encourage students to do revisions on an essay, so we should allow reworking of other assignments and, yes, even some assessments.

> **All students deserve "whatever it takes" to help them become the most successful student possible.**

When students have a chance to learn from their mistakes and redo or rewrite, not only do they often do better in terms of scores or academic accomplishment, they also experience increases in hope, motivation, and growth mindset. These second (and third and fourth) chances teach students that failure sometimes happens, that failure isn't the end but instead is the first step toward growth, and that failure doesn't define them.

Middle level consultant and author Rick Wormeli (2011) addresses this topic in the article, "Redos and Retakes Done Right: Allowing Students to Redo Assignments and Assessments Is the Best Way to Prepare Them for Adult Life." He reminds teachers, "The goal is that all students learn the content, not just the ones who can learn on the uniform timeline. Curriculum goals don't require that every individual reaches the same level of proficiency on the same day, only that every student achieves the goal" (p. 23).

If you don't already do so, start the practice of allowing (and even encouraging) second chances on assignments and assessments (for full credit). Before you start, however, set up your criteria for redos and retakes—in what cases this can happen, how they will be assessed, how much time a student has, how many do-overs a student can have, and what kind of agreement you'll have ahead of time with the student (and in some cases, with parents also). Make it clear that any redo or retake is at the teacher's discretion, but be careful to exercise that discretion equitably. Be sure that you and the student compare the final "do" with the original try to see the student's progress.

Also, do more research about this topic and how to do it well (and how not to do it). We recommend that you read Wormeli's entire 2011 article (mentioned above) for a discussion of this, including 14 practical tips on managing redos. He also gives advice on this topic in a 2016 article on the Middleweb site (Wormeli, 2016a) and a 2010 YouTube video.

When we look back at the many attitudes and practices—along with the long lists of skills to teach—suggested in this chapter, we're reminded again of the complexity of the process of *becoming* capable at both academic and personal skills. We're also reminded again of how incredible and harmonious is this partnership between *becoming* and *belonging*. With all that educators know about the interrelatedness of our students' personal, social, emotional, ethical, and cognitive development and needs, still the priority is often placed on academic achievement (generally measured by test scores or grades). This choice ignores the awesome network of qualities and assets that contribute to academic achievement and to a whole, well-functioning person. An emphasis on one or the other (academics or personal development) doesn't work, because there is no separation. All the positive, productive, healthy attributes students need to develop are imbedded in both!

Putting It into Practice

As an individual, team, small group, or entire staff, use some of these activities to spark discussions, reflect on your current practices or situations, listen to others, or set goals.

1. Examine how your school's master schedule affects students' opportunities to take exploratory classes. How many elective classes does your school offer? Do students have choice of classes? Does the schedule force students to lose time in non-academic classes if additional assistance or catch-up work is needed in academic classes? Are there opportunities for students to explore areas of interest outside of formal classes (mini-courses, brown-bag lunch groups, clubs, etc.)? How can the schedule and other exploration opportunities be improved to allow students access to all classes, particularly areas of interest that are most meaningful to them?

2. Examine school practices and policies regarding student participation in activities based on academic performance. Are students restricted or prevented from participating in a course or activity if they are not passing in a required content area course? Do coaches or club leaders work together with teachers to encourage students to do better in academic classes? Is there consistency across the staff in how these practices are implemented? Is any consideration given to a student's work ethic or what the student **did** learn over final academic performance?

3. Group Discussion: Review your school's procedures for allowing re-teaching and redos. Is this a common practice in your school? Do all teachers participate? Is it mandatory or voluntary? Is there consistency? If there are no established procedures, discuss the need for developing procedures and what they might look like if created.

4. Download the Schools to Watch Rubric from the National Forum to Accelerate Middle-Grades Reform website (www.middlegradesforum.org). Individually complete the "Academically Excellent" section of the rubric. Tally the scores. Use the results as a springboard for a discussion about how your school meets the criteria.

Chapter 7

Honor and Foster Student Voice and Choice

"Teachers who find their kids' ideas fascinating are just better teachers than teachers who find the subject matter fascinating."

- Philip Sadler

At a Convention on the Rights of the Child in 1989, the United Nations General Assembly passed a resolution internationally verifying that each child has "the right to express his or her views freely in all matters affecting the child, the views of the child being given due weight in accordance with the age and maturity of the child" (Article 12, Part 1).

What is more fundamental to *belonging* in any setting and *becoming* in any pursuit than this right to express one's views freely in matters affecting oneself? And what is more essential to the foundations of our mission as educators than the beliefs and values that lead us to honor and attend to this right? For beneath any actions to welcome and nurture the voices of our students lies a belief that **all** of them have not only the right, but the capabilities and wisdom to identify their interests and need to express their opinions and perspectives, and to take part in important decisions that affect their lives at school.

Student voice: In the school context, the idea of *voice* for students refers to the extent to which students are able and free to express their viewpoints, values, opinions, suggestions, and personal experiences and backgrounds. But voice goes beyond expression. If we acknowledge that students are people with rights, then we must respect what they say. In a school, voice includes the degree to which students' expressions are listened to, valued, taken seriously, considered, and acted upon when making decisions about their instruction and other aspects of their school lives. It includes the level of students' involvement and investment in the life of the school.

Student choice: The concept of *choice* in the school involves a setting wherein students have options in the practices of the classroom and school, including in their learning experiences. But the concept goes further than just options. Student choice at its best means that students have meaningful, relevant choices, choices that are not just selections from a list of options, but choices that involve a student's action and participation and that support development of the student's autonomy and competence.

> **Student choice is inherent in the definition of student voice. Voice only truly exists where there is choice.**

Voice and Choice: *Student choice* is inherent in the definition of *student voice*. Voice only truly exists where there is choice. And offering choice automatically involves and leads to honoring and encouraging voice. An environment where students have many opportunities for choice communicates to students that their voices matter. Together, these concepts affirm that students **do** have insights into and interest in their own learning and **can** make meaningful decisions about the design of their own learning and school environment. Fostering both voice and choice is a smart way to draw students into active participation in their own *belonging* and *becoming*.

Honoring and Fostering Voice

Why?

We start from the truth that each student deserves to be heard. That is the foremost reason for honoring and fostering student voice. In addition, benefits abound when we offer students authentic and constructive ways to express themselves and take an active role in making decisions—benefits for students and all those who work with them. Research has linked student voice positively to a number of the very aspects of *belonging* and *becoming* that are critical to students' well-being and success in school and to school improvement (Arnot, 2003; Beaudoin, 2005; Cook-Sather, 2002, 2006; Fielding, 2001, 2004; Flutter, 2007; Flutter & Ruddick, 2004; Fredricks, Blumenfeld, & Paris, 2004; MacBeath, Demetriou, Rudduck, & Myers, 2003; McIntyre, Pedder, Ruddick, 2005; Mitra, 2004; Pedder, 2009; Pedder & McIntyre, 2006; Rudduck & McIntyre, 2007). Schools report the same such results when they focus on developing student voice. In summary, here are some of the outcomes and changes that have been found in the presence of meaningful practices to elevate student voice:

- **Students learn better. Achievement increases.**

    Motivation and engagement increase.

    Students shift into active roles as shapers of their education.

    Students get involved in learning processes in ways they might not have before.

    Students are more committed to what they're learning.

    Students are more willing to take on academic challenges.

    Exploration and curiosity increase.

    Students believe in themselves more.

Students take more initiative and grow in autonomy.

Students perceive themselves as increasing in competence.

Students gain confidence and a sense that their ideas make a difference.

Learning is perceived as more relevant.

Students take on more responsibility for their learning.

Students gain a sense of themselves as learners.

Leadership abilities increase.

The sense of being worthwhile and doing something worthwhile grows.

Learning becomes more diverse as diverse voices are heard.

- **Students feel a greater sense of *belonging* to their school and classes.**

Students identify more with school programs and events.

Students are more likely to get involved in classroom and school activities.

Attitudes about school improve.

As students hear each other's voices, they learn more about each other.

As students listen to each other, opportunities to value and respect each other increase.

Relationships with peers improve.

Students feel more valued by teachers.

Student attendance improves.

- **Teachers teach better.**

Learning is redefined as a joint venture between students and teachers.

Teachers see more positive attitudes in their classrooms (and often, in themselves).

Teachers learn more about their students.

Teachers learn from their students.

Teachers find that their relationships with students deepen.

Teachers get insights into students' ideas and capabilities.

Teachers learn more about how individual students think and learn.

Teachers are better able to plan effective learning for and with students.

Teachers learn more about how their teaching is working.

Teachers learn about students' understanding or misconceptions of concepts.

Teachers are more excited about learning.

Teacher attendance improves.

How?

Much has been discussed about how to give voice to students. But in reality, we educators can't **give** voice to our students; each human being already has a voice. We give honor to their voices. We give messages about the value of their voices. We give priority to listening to and learning from their voices. We create and give opportunities for their voices to be heard. We give students structures and supports that help them strengthen their own voices. And we give ourselves to acting on what we learn from them. Instead of asking how to give voice to students, we should ask, "What do we do with the voices our students bring to us?"

Researchers Barbara McCombs and Jo Ann Whisler (1997) are advocates of the learner-centered classroom and its success at increasing student motivation and achievement. We can't help but notice that every part of their description of a learner-centered classroom (or school) connects to the concept of how to enhance student voice. They have defined the term *learner-centered* as beliefs, characteristics, dispositions, and practices of teachers that

(1) include learners in decisions about how and what they learn and how that learning is assessed;

(2) take each learner's unique perspectives seriously and consider these perspectives part of the learning probes;

(3) respect and accommodate individual differences in learners' backgrounds, interests, abilities, and experiences; and

(4) treat learners as co-creators in the teaching and learning process (p. 33).

When we consider the kinds of actions and strategies to recommend to our readers, we are, first, inspired to share the words of Benjamin Levin (2000), who researches the role of student voice in school improvement (and ardently believes that students **must** be at the center of school improvement efforts). Levin said that we must "make it normal, even expected, that students would have a reasoned, informed, and respected voice in school decisions" (p. 172).

In its beginning or minimal form, fostering of student voice means that students give ideas or opinions when they are asked to do so (without a promise that anyone will act on their ideas). At its best and most complex, it "calls for a cultural shift that opens up spaces and minds not only to the sound but also to the presence and power of students" (Cook-Sather, 2006, p. 363). In every aspect, from simplest to most complex, student voice is an important part of school culture.

What schools and teachers believe about students' wisdom and abilities to take active roles in their own education will be reflected in the level of voice in a school or classroom. But it is not just the belief that makes the difference. In fact, it could be argued that the belief isn't real if there is no action to improve the level of student voice. There are unlimited strategies for taking action that fosters student voice. Here are some practices to explore and expand as you work to increase the level and positive impact of student voice:

Do-able steps—Start from where you are and plan to take one step at a time toward increasing the level of student voice. But wherever you are and whatever your goals, always keep these truths as a part of your belief system and let the beliefs show in your attitudes and actions: Students have the right to be heard. They deserve respect for their ideas, interests, and opinions. They have ideas worthy of being included in decisions and plans. You can learn from students. Middle level students are full of new cognitive powers, hunger for autonomy, boundless curiosity, and questions—non-stop questions. We can let this drive us crazy, or we can corral these developmental characteristics into meaningful expressions of voice that include students in making important decisions and contributions. And we must "make it normal" that they do so.

Interactive teaching—Plan to include some expression of student voice in every lesson with lots of discussion (in pairs, small and large groups on many topics, academic and otherwise); frequent student response as the lesson is developed; questions and answers (students, as well as the teacher, doing the questioning and answering); periodic feedback; and intermittent review of what they've learned and understood.

Voice-friendly instructional methods—Plan to involve students in such endeavors as exploration, inquiry, experimentation, student-led conferences, peer mentoring, and argumentative writing and speaking (and formal or informal debate).

Interactive management—Make sure student ideas and experiences are a part of classroom protocols. Give students as much responsibility as possible for designing and managing procedures in the classroom.

Discussion—Make room and time for discussions on many topics—interesting intellectual ideas (students can initiate by sharing something they heard or learned or wonder), questions, social issues, classroom learning, or classroom life.

Connections—Before, during, and after learning activities, have students make connections to their experiences, to things they already know, to what is important in their lives, to how the new skill or information can be applied to other contexts. You can give them a few minutes to complete such statements as "This connects to . . . ," "I could see this working with . . . ," or "This is relevant to my life because . . .".

Feedback—Find many ways for students to give and receive feedback. Ask for frequent questions or comments on classroom procedures and lessons. Stop during lessons and ask what they're wondering about, what they're hearing, what they understand, or what they see as important. Have them summarize what they've learned by telling each other, demonstrating it, writing it in a journal, or putting it onto a sticky note or in a Tweet or text message.

Collaborative learning—Make collaborative pairs or groups a standard part of the learning in your classroom. When students work together (having been taught appropriate ways to do so), their voices are used and heard. They grow in understanding and appreciation of each other. They learn the subject and learn about each other.

Research—Provide chances for students to gather information and viewpoints on important topics (classroom or school policies, for example), summarize what they learn, draw conclusions and consider implications, present their findings, and use their findings to make suggestions related to school concerns.

Reflection—Include daily reflection on such things as their goal attainment, learning outcomes, thinking processes, questions, confusions, work progress, specific learning experiences, or conditions and experiences in the classroom. They can do this on reflection forms or in journals.

Goal setting and attainment—Student voice is elevated when they set their own goals, articulate their goals, design and carry out plans to meet the goals, and evaluate their outcomes and processes.

Inclusion on school governing bodies—Commit to the idea that students are valuable contributors to decision-making groups in the school. Realize that, in fact, students offer perspectives, information, and ideas that can't be gained from any other source—and it's a loss to make decisions without that input. Bring students into team meetings, faculty meetings, staff leadership team meetings, and even school board meetings. See that there is student representation on school councils, task forces, and information-gathering committees.

Choice—Offer middle level students an ongoing selection of choices in all aspects of their school lives. See more on this later in the chapter.

Top 8 Ways to Foster Voice

- Ask for their perceptions, opinions, feedback, and ideas. Listen. Take them seriously.

- Plan for students to interact with you and each other during lessons.

- Include students on school governing bodies.

- Use student surveys that enable them to share reflections, opinions, evaluations, and ideas anonymously.

- Give students ways to reflect frequently on what and how they've learned.

- Put students in charge wherever and whenever possible. They are capable of this—probably more than you think.

- Use them as "expert witnesses" of teaching and learning. They know things you don't!

- When you invite student voice, act on what you learn from students.

Students in charge—Shift some of the power. Nurture students' autonomy and responsibility. Let students take charge of classroom procedures, decisions, tasks, and teaching wherever possible, workable, and appropriate for their developmental level. (Don't underestimate what they are capable of doing responsibly.)

Teaching the teacher—Student voice researchers Julia Flutter and Jean Ruddick (2004) heartily recommend using students as "expert witnesses" of teaching and learning, because students are keen observers of school life and have valuable insights to offer (p. 4). Ask students to describe the content, concept, skill, or process they've learned. Ask them to describe and evaluate how and what you've taught. Ask them to redesign a lesson you are planning to teach or have taught. Ask them to tell you how they learn best. Ask them to share observations about what works and doesn't work in the classroom.

Student-led parent-teacher conferences—One of the most meaningful experiences students can have in exercising voice happens when students plan and lead parent conferences. We've mentioned this before, but the process is so voice-centered that we needed to mention it again. With some teacher guidance or an agreed-upon list of contents, students choose what evidence of their progress, performance, and passions in their school lives to show their parents. They also choose how to present it and what to say. In short, they are the designers and implementers of their own conferences.

Seeking and Listening to Students' Perceptions and Opinions

When I (Patti) was a middle school principal, our district passed a bond levy that provided for a budget that included money for new playground structures at the elementary schools. I lobbied hard, and despite some district-level skepticism that young adolescents would view it as "babyish" and it would go unused, got the go-ahead to have a playground structure built for the middle school. Realizing that the older students might be the hardest to sell on the idea, I set up a task force selected at random (to assure a mixed group). I gave them catalogs of playground equipment and asked them to design a structure that students would use. They came up with a plan, worked with the contractor to incorporate their ideas, and watched as the structure was built. The first day the new structure was open for student use, it was swarmed, as the counselor remarked, "...like ants on Terro (a liquid ant killer)." The students' plan was a hit with all grade levels; all it took for a successful outcome was asking students for input.

"Whose voice is heard in this school?" This is a question for all educators to ask. What happens in schools and classrooms is most often the result of adult decision-making—decisions handed down from the district office, from administrators, or from teachers or other staff. The nature of organizing and planning in a school (master schedules, programs, supervision duty, school-improvement processes) lends itself to school being an adult-decision-dominated world. Our earlier discussion gave many reasons why it is critical to bring students into these processes. We know that when students believe they matter and that their perspectives and suggestions matter, they are much more likely to engage in learning processes. And we know that as the level of student voice rises, so does the level of teaching, learning, and personal development in a school and its classrooms.

The most basic actions resulting from our commitment to student voice are asking to hear it and listening to what we hear. We can't assume that students will automatically say what they need to say or what we need to hear. Because many young adolescents believe that school is about adults and not about them or perhaps because they have not been taught to advocate for themselves, they aren't comfortable speaking their thoughts. Even for those students who do speak up, it's not enough to wait for them to bring ideas or share concerns of their own volition.

As the authors, we in no way wish to minimize all the efforts already underway in schools to support and develop student voice or power. We know that schools have student councils and student leadership groups that do great work coordinating food drives, spirit weeks, school dances, and other (very important) school events. However, many times these traditional student organizations don't provide enough opportunities for students to give consistent and meaningful input to decision-making in their school. And they don't always include **all** students. Teachers and administrators must actively seek out **all** students' opinions and insights to learn their perceptions about their classrooms and about the school outside the classroom doors.

To offer the best chances to elevate voice for all students, educators must create specific strategies, initiatives, and tools to gain ideas, information, and evaluations from students. These can take such forms as

- Task forces.
- Interviews (peer-peer, student-teacher, teacher-student with results shared).
- Periodic student evaluations of learning experiences.
- Periodic student evaluations of classes.
- Daily or weekly journal entries with reflections on the week's learning.
- Questionnaires (created by students or teachers).
- Student surveys (created by students or teachers).
- Ongoing processes for students to give feedback.
- Student committees to research and address school issues.
- Long-term or short-term student decision-making groups.
- Student presentations to school governing bodies.
- Student membership in school governing bodies.

These are other strategies we've found to give powerful representation to—and action influenced by—student voice:

Students Working with the Board of Trustees—When I (Laurie) moved into the role of district superintendent and my daily interaction with students diminished, I was challenged to find meaningful ways to directly gain input from students. Inspired by a strategy modeled by a colleague, we began (and have continued) a practice of hosting student-led district board work sessions. In each session, ten groups of students have an opportunity to "make a pitch" for their ideas for school and district improvement. Their audience is school board members, administrators, teachers, and parents. The results have been astounding. Students have learned valuable skills, their voices have been heard, and their sense of *belonging* to their school and district has soared. Equally important, the adults have learned from the students in ways they never imagined. An article I wrote for *AMLE Magazine* (Barron, 2015) explains this process and tells the story more fully. See the entire article "Students Take the Lead," (Appendix E) on pages 239–241 in this book.

A Student Leadership Council—The staff in the middle school where I (Laurie) was principal found another exciting way to elicit student wisdom. We drew on a mixed group of students specifically for the purpose of hearing student voice in ways that would lead to students being a force in school improvement. We formed a Student Leadership Council that gave 30 diverse students responsibilities for listening to their peers and then forming plans for addressing students' concerns. Through research, good communication, taking the pulse of the school, and designing creative solutions and actions, students on the council took part in serious decision-making and effected important changes. Since the 30 students on the council drew opinions from the entire student body, all students' voices were strengthened. As a side effect, all of the students on the council showed many gains in personal autonomy, competence, and leadership skills. Some students made amazing turnarounds from negative to positive directions in their attitudes and behaviors. For the full story and description of the council, see the article, "Student Leadership Council," (Appendix D) on pages 237–238 in this book.

Student Surveys—Student surveys are highly effective tools for gathering student perspectives and advice. (Students generally like doing these, especially when they are anonymous.) Teachers or schools can create a survey to gain ideas or feedback on a single topic or several topics. A survey can be specific to one classroom, a grade-level, a team, or an entire school. Any survey that asks students to reflect on their school experience is an opportunity to honor and learn from student voice. With easy-to-access survey tools such as Google Forms and Survey Monkey, teachers can develop many kinds of surveys. A middle level classroom teacher might design a survey with such categories and statements as these (to which students answer *strongly agree, somewhat agree, somewhat disagree, or strongly disagree*):

- Relationships
  - My teacher knows and cares about me as a student and a person.
  - My teacher values and respects me as an individual.
- Relevance
  - I can apply what I learn in this class to the real world.
  - I understand how I can apply what I learn in this class to something in my life either now or in my future.
- Rigor
  - My classwork is challenging.
  - Most of the classwork my teacher assigns requires me to apply what I have learned, solve problems, and really think about what I have learned.

There are dozens of categories and purposes for student surveys. Teachers can design questions or statements to discover student perceptions about how time is used in a class, if the teacher explains concepts in several different ways to give lots of chances for understanding, if students find the class engaging, if students' ideas and suggestions are valued, if students are treated fairly, or if students have easy ways to get help when they need it. Surveys can provide information about students' sense of *belonging*, whether they perceive the class is increasing their competence, if they are encouraged (and trusted) to learn independently, what instructional methods fit them best, how

The ultimate goal of using surveys is for teachers and other staff members to obtain meaningful feedback that will lead them to examine and reflect upon their effectiveness in the classroom or school.

the school (or class) reflects and encourages diversity, if they feel they are gaining what they need to *become* successful in high school and beyond school, and any number of other topics. Student voice is elevated even more, by the way, when students help create the surveys!

The ultimate goal of using surveys is for teachers and other staff members to obtain meaningful feedback that will lead them to examine and reflect upon their effectiveness in the classroom or school. Knowing how students feel about each of these areas can help classroom teachers and schools set improvement goals for areas that will increase students' success at *belonging* and *becoming*.

Student surveys can also be accessed online. The Quaglia Institute for School Voice & Aspirations has surveys that target student voice, teacher voice, and parent voice. The Student Voice Survey (Corwin & Quaglia, 2017) measures eight conditions in a school that affect student voice. It is based on *The 8 Conditions that Make a Difference*® that "help educators ensure that the work they are already doing fosters an environment characterized by positive relationships, engaged learning, and sense of purpose" (Quaglia, 2017). These eight conditions are:

1. Belonging
2. Heroes
3. Sense of Accomplishment
4. Fun & Excitement
5. Curiosity & Creativity
6. Spirit of Adventure
7. Leadership & Responsibility
8. Confidence to Take Action

Students rate their level of agreement (from *strongly agree* to *strongly disagree*) to a series of statements related to each of the above eight conditions in their school. Other online organizations, such as the Search Institute, offer a range of surveys with which teachers can listen to student voices. Knowing students' perceptions about each of these conditions identified in surveys can help guide us as we work to nurture these conditions in our schools.

Student input on classes and teaching style can give us information we can't get from test scores. It might even help us know what that test score will be before students take the test, as students' perceptions tend to mirror their achievement results. If students are telling you something's not right, they are probably correct, and their achievement results will likely reflect that same perception.

With both school and classroom level surveys, it's helpful to get feedback while you can still use it. Issuing student perception surveys on the first day students return to school after winter break provides enough time for school leaders and teachers to gather and then actually use the feedback they get to benefit students. This midpoint of the year is an ideal time to get feedback (especially when students are fresh from a school break, had no homework due that morning, and are still thinking about holiday fun and not how their teacher perhaps made them angry before the break).

For more ideas about questions to ask and topics to discuss with students, we suggest you read Kathleen Cushman's (2009) book, *Fires in the Middle School Bathroom: Advice for Teachers from Middle Schoolers*. Cushman traveled around the country to record the voices of middle school students, asking them questions and engaging them in discussions about their lives and learning in middle school, and the advice they want teachers to hear. Her aim, she said, was "first and foremost to attune the teacher to the rewards of listening closely to students themselves" (p. 6).

Making It Safe for Students to Share Their Opinions

If we are to encourage students to openly share their input, then it must be done in a safe environment, particularly if their perceptions are ones they find difficult to share. Taking any risk, whether as a student or an adult, always opens the possibility of failure or embarrassment. If a student shares an opinion and is met with ridicule by the adult (or other students), it is probable that the student will avoid sharing opinions in the future. Thus, when we invite student voice, we must be sure that it happens in a positive school culture that permeates all classrooms, supporting risk-taking and free (appropriate) expression of their viewpoints.

- Give students ways to offer opinions in private (anonymous surveys or questionnaires provide a safety net for students to share perceptions with "those who are in charge," particularly if the questions are about "those who are in charge"). Honor this privacy. Ask permission for sharing any student comments that are not anonymous.
- Establish guidelines within the class and school about how opinions are to be received and welcomed.
- Work to see that the adults in the school set a strong precedent for responding to opinions (students' and other adults') with respect.
- Teach students how to share and listen to each other's opinions respectfully—without ridicule or negative comments. Practice this in the classroom often.
- Consistently remind students that, even if others disagree with them, they still have value as people and their opinions still have value.
- Honor the value of student voice by responding when they take the risk of speaking or writing their opinions. Thank them for their reflections, information, and ideas. Tell them specifically what you learned from them and how they were helpful.

Acting on Students' Perceptions and Opinions

Student perception data is equally as important as the academic data typically collected by schools and teachers. Yes, we also dislike the four-letter D word at times. However, with all of the data out there to help guide continuous improvement, many schools still don't gather their most accessible data (and data, by the way, that is the least expensive to analyze): students' perceptions and opinions. As educators, we are always looking at data. We talk constantly about data-driven decisions. Yet, are we reviewing student perceptions even half as much as we review their test scores? (We would guess that the answer in most schools is "no.")

There is a difference between being listened to and being listened to with respect and taken seriously. There is a difference between taking students' voices seriously and taking authentic, concrete actions to use the knowledge we get from listening to students. This is true about all situations in which you seek students' thoughts and experiences or in which students initiate sharing their voice. This is true for a student's brief statement analyzing which learning strategies best help her learn to solve equations. It is true for the presentation a group of students gives before the school board to argue in favor of a change in detention policies. For any instance of students expressing their voices, the greatest value comes from what happens next.

> **There is a difference between being listened to and being listened to with respect and taken seriously.**

Be aware that what you **do** with the results of a student survey has a greater effect on students *belonging* and *becoming* and on raising the level of student voice (or not raising it, or lowering it) than does the students' satisfaction at getting to express their opinions in the first place. If a student takes the risk of sharing an idea, opinion, or experience and there is no response—or if there is some affirming verbal response but nothing further happens, she'll get the message that the expression was not worth the risk. Unfortunately, this happens all too often. We ask for students' opinions, we get them, but they go nowhere. And students don't ever learn why nothing seemed to happen. Before we ask to hear from students, we should have a plan for what we'll do with the information they give.

Take students' reasonable suggestions about procedures and learning in the classroom and find ways to integrate them into or replace current practices. Bring student ideas relating to wider school topics to teams, committees, administrators, or boards that make decisions on the matters. (Better yet, arrange for students to present their honed ideas themselves). We should never ask for student suggestions or opinions without taking action, letting students know what was done with the information they gave, and making sure that at least a lot of the time, their voices made a difference, changed something, or made something better. They must see some of their ideas put into action. They must get feedback on what we learned from them. This is the best way to affirm student voice and to raise the level of its expression.

Teaching Students to Appropriately Share Opinions and Respond to Feedback

When we seek student's opinions, we must not assume that they know how to give them. Expressing one's voice—one's closely-held beliefs, creative ideas, opinions, and evaluations—involves a host of personal, academic, and social skills. Teachers must teach students how to share opinions clearly, appropriately, respectfully, and in ways that make them likely to be heard and make a difference. We must help students see that yelling across the room that a test "is stupid" is neither an appropriate nor productive way to share input (even if they do, in fact, think the test is stupid). They need to know that an opinion shared in that manner is likely to be disregarded. When students have opportunities to be heard, it's pretty impressive how appropriate, mature, and thoughtful they can be (all aspects we want to see in a student who is growing toward *becoming* a young adult). We owe it to students to teach them skills that will enable their voices to be heard in the most satisfying and effective ways possible.

To elevate student voice in positive, compelling ways, we must help students learn and polish skills of speaking, writing, and listening. They need to learn and practice argumentation, skills of researching (to find evidence to support opinions, where necessary), organizing, reasoning, collaborating, reflecting, and discussing. They need to learn and practice such personal and social skills as respect, politeness, kindness, tolerance, suspension of judgment, authenticity, patience, open-mindedness, self-regulation, and impulse control (aspects content standards alone cannot teach). Most of these skills and behaviors we already incorporate into our classes and other school activities. They can be honed and reinforced through mini-lessons, role-playing, and class discussions.

Back before Oregon had statewide laws prohibiting smoking on school grounds and at school activities, students who had been studying the impact of secondhand smoke in their health classes came to me, the principal (Patti), with an idea. While no smoking was allowed in the school building, they explained that spectators coming to outdoor events like football and soccer would smoke, often while standing behind the players on sidelines. The students didn't like others smoking on campus and wanted it banned. With the guidance of their teachers who mentored them on the steps, skills, and behaviors needed, students created a presentation to take to the school board, requested time on the agenda, and went before the board to plead their case. (By the way, imagine the research, writing, speaking, respect, anxiety control, argumentation, and other skills needed to prepare and execute this plan!)

Help students understand that when their suggestions are not implemented, it does not mean that they were not heard or their opinions not valued.

The school board listened and agreed to discuss and consider their request. After doing so over the course of a few months, the board implemented a policy that prohibited smoking on all school grounds and at all school-sponsored activities. The students had a good reason to celebrate and a good lesson on how to address a concern and request changes in an appropriate manner.

It is equally important to help students understand that when their suggestions are not implemented, it does not mean that they were not heard or their opinion not valued. For example, a common concern of middle school students is that lunch is too short. (Sometimes teachers feel the same way!) Students are not usually aware of scheduling complexities, class-time requirements, and other regulations that make it impossible to extend a lunch period even by a few minutes. But, they need to know about these kinds of complications. Explain the behind-the-scenes details that affect the issues they bring up. Don't underestimate their ability to understand complexities. These complexities are the stuff of real life and good information for them to have.

Acknowledge students' arguments (which may even be valid), paraphrase their concerns, and explain the constraints that may prohibit satisfying their wishes. These actions will go a long way toward helping students feel they were heard than if they get a simple "no, we can't do that" answer. Many times, we owe students far more of an explanation than we are willing to give. We honor student voice, as well as their maturity and capabilities, when we take the time to explain.

In summary, when we listen to students' voices and use what we learn from them, our classrooms and schools are better for our students and for ourselves. Let us find ways to honor and listen to what every student can teach us! As Adam Fletcher, avid advocate for student voice, said, "Student voice is only as strong as the least engaged student" (2003a).

Honoring and Fostering Choice

Why?

We honor and foster student choice for the same reasons we honor student voice. As humans, students deserve to have a say in their lives in and outside of school, and choice is a primary component of voice. It's a vehicle through which students can be agents of their own learning and of many other processes of their *belonging* and *becoming*. A student does not have a meaningful role (with any sense that her or his contributions actually make a difference) in learning or classroom life when everything that student does in school happens at the direction of a teacher (the teacher chooses the topics, sets the goals, makes the rules, prescribes the exact path to reach the goal, decides all the outcomes, decides the consequences, and designs the assessments). Even as adults, we tend to be more accepting of ideas, more eager to finish a task, more willing to take on additional workloads, if we are given some form of choice in how those things are completed. Thus, just as we must take students' perceptions and opinions seriously, we must also take seriously the importance of allowing students some (appropriate) self-direction over work they are asked to do.

As with other efforts to elevate student voice, a school environment that offers meaningful choices for students is positively linked to many aspects of *belonging* and *becoming*. Increases are found in such qualities and characteristics as autonomy, intrinsic motivation, engagement, self-efficacy, self-determination, self-regulation, self-esteem, task effort, perceived competence, achievement, cognitive flexibility, curiosity, creativity, interest in school, trust of teachers, comfortable relationships with peers, sense of *belonging*, and general well-being at school. Students who have choices take more initiative in school processes and learning opportunities. When they can pursue their own interests and questions, students find learning to be more relevant and they make better use of their own talents and strengths. When we give students choices, they get the message that we believe in their competence to make decisions and succeed. This respect inspires them to take more responsibility for their own learning and *become* even more competent. When they have choices in what they learn and how to learn it, students are more willing to take on challenges and to persist and finish tasks. When students have choices regarding classroom rules and procedures, they are more likely to follow them. (Assor, Kaplan, & Roth, 2002; Cornelius-White, 2007; Deci and Ryan, 1987; Fredricks, Blumenfeld, & Paris, 2004; Katz & Assor, 2006; McCombs & Whisler, 1997; Patall, Cooper, & Robinson, 2008; Patall, Cooper, & Wynn, 2010; Reeve, Jang, Carrell, Jeon, & Barch 2004; Reeve, Nix, & Hamm, 2003).

What?

To enhance voice, autonomy, and other aspects of *becoming*, students should have appropriate, meaningful choices in

- What they learn.
- How they learn.
- How they will work (alone, with others).
- Where they learn.
- With whom they learn.
- Specific learning tasks.
- Tools for learning (resources, technology, etc.).
- Homework assignments.
- Ways to gain new information and skills.
- Ways to practice and expand skills.
- Ways to expand and deepen knowledge.
- Ways to explain their thinking and learning processes.
- How they show what they learn.
- How they show mastery of a concept or skill.
- How they are evaluated on what they learn.
- What goals they set.
- Making plans for attaining a goal.
- Timelines for their goals.
- Classroom (or team) rules, processes, and procedures.
- Implementation of classroom rules and procedures.
- Evaluation of classroom rules and procedures.
- Some school policies.
- Options for choices.

How?

Here are some suggestions and ideas to consider as you embrace and expand the commitment to integrating student choice into classroom and school life:

Believe in students' ability to choose. Believe that your middle level students are capable of self-determined, autonomous learning and of the cognitive and self-regulation skills that will enable them to take an active part in their own learning and classroom life. Show your belief by giving them real choices. They are more likely to use these capabilities when they feel some control over their learning.

Model making wise choices. The best way to teach students how to make wise choices is to show them. Talk through the processes of gathering (or examining) options, weighing options, looking for options that relate to your own interests or skills (or answer your questions), deciding which options are reasonable or doable, discarding those that are too easy or beyond moderately challenging. Let them watch and listen to you make and follow through on choices. Talk about figures from history, literature, or current events who have made wise (or unwise) choices.

Teach the skills needed for choice. Along with your belief that they are capable of making choices, give students instruction in how to do it. Teach them the skills that support autonomy, decision-making, self-determination. Be sure to plan ongoing mini lessons that help them learn to break down learning tasks into manageable steps; define, set, and articulate attainable goals; make a plan to attain a goal; identify their own interests and capabilities; make reasonable choices; organize tasks to meet a goal; monitor their progress as they work; collaborate with others to solve problems and make decisions; ask for help when they need it; and learn other skills they'll need to be successful with the choices they make.

Offer meaningful choices. When choices meet students' needs for autonomy, competence, and relatedness (in harmony with their cultural values), students are motivated and engaged (Katz & Assor, 2006; Assor, Kaplan, & Roth, 2002; Patall, Cooper, & Wynn, 2010). Having options that are tied to their individual questions, curiosities, interests, strengths, abilities, and real lives inspires students to work hard. This supports their intrinsic motivation and shows that you know them, understand them, and respect their preferences. It invites students to invest themselves in quality work that matters. To gain the benefits possible with student choice, the choices must be relevant and, thus, meaningful.

Offer real choices. When an assignment says, "Solve ten of the twenty practice problems on the worksheet" or "Answer every other question at the end of the chapter," there is no boost given to students' autonomy or competence. Patal, Cooper, and Wynn (2010) refer to the importance of "action choices." These are choices in how to do something, rather than choices of which items to complete from a list the teacher provides. The positive effects of choice are stronger when students are not just choosing among teacher-generated different versions of the same task (Patall, Cooper, & Robinson, 2008).

> When an assignment says, "Solve ten of the twenty practice problems on the worksheet" or "Answer every other question at the end of the chapter," there is no boost given to students' autonomy or competence.

Don't overcomplicate the choices. We've listed many areas for kinds of choices. Students don't have to be making all those choices at once. Your students may progress to a project for which students choose what, how, where, when, with whom, and on what timeline they learn—and also go on to choose how the learning will be assessed. But each one of these choices is valuable in itself. These kinds of choices can (and should) be practiced one at a time.

Don't shy away from small choices. Choices can be big or small. Every choice doesn't have to be a major choice. Students need many, many experiences making small choices. Sometimes the choice involves a small assignment in which a student pursues a personal interest or explores something that has sparked her curiosity. As long as the choice is meaningful, it is worthwhile. These can be worked into every facet of classroom life and learning. There are many situations and decisions in a school day when teachers can offer students clear, simple options for choice.

Keep choices challenging. To be effective for learning and growth, a choice must be complex, but not too hard. Offer choices that are challenging enough to build competence but not so difficult or complex that they are beyond the possibility of students reaching them. When you're preparing options for a class assignment, you'll need to include a range of difficulty. But help each student choose a moderately challenging option. If the options are relevant to a student's interests, she or he will be willing to take on the challenge.

Make the requirements clear. With any choices—whether it be about academics, policies, procedures, behaviors, or planning events—students must know what is expected. There may be a variety of ways to get to the goal, but we can't expect students to get there if they don't know what the goal is. Be sure that students can state the requirement, i.e., "Demonstrate that you can solve a multistep equation with two variables when one variable is known" or "Introduce a claim and support it with logical reasoning and relevant evidence from credible sources" or "Choose a way and time to do your classroom job. Just be sure that the end result of doing it fulfills the job description."

Connect academic choices to clear standards. As teachers, it's our responsibility to ensure that curriculum, instruction, and assessment practices lead students to mastery of the standards. When another goal is to increase student voice and choice, plan your instruction to offer choices in some aspects of working toward a standard. Be sure that the complexity of the choices matches the complexity of the curriculum standard.

For example, there are multiple ways a student can show mastery of a reading standard such as "cite evidence from a text that analyzes what the text says explicitly and implicitly." (There is a standard similar to this for middle level students in every state.) For choices, students might choose to work on the standard through two of the following: describing development of the main character, identifying the theme, showing the author's purpose, exposing author bias, summarizing the key conflict or claim of the text, analyzing literary devices used, or showing relevance of the information to real life. Students can also choose **how** they will show mastery; they could select from such options as writing an essay or song lyrics, drawing cartoons or diagrams, giving a speech, acting out a scene (with citations from the text), giving a TV-style news report, joining with another student to hold a debate, or creating and showing a media presentation using any number of presentation tools found online or on computers.

Top 8 Ways to Foster Choice

- Believe that students are capable of making choices about their learning and school lives.

- Teach students skills they need for making appropriate choices.

- Offer real, not manufactured, choices—choices that involve their action.

- Give students choices in what to learn, how they learn, and how they show what they learn.

- Make choice a normal, frequent part of classroom life.

- Let students create the choices.

- Offer choices that are meaningful and relevant to students' lives and interests.

- Offer choices that are challenging, but not out of reach.

The important point here is that, regardless of the choices for ways to work on the standard and demonstrate mastery, **all students are working toward the same standard.** That is the clear goal. But in taking some control over the process, students will be more engaged with the material, put more effort toward completing it, and find more enjoyment and meaning in their work. As a result, students are far more likely to master the standard than if they had no ownership in the assignment.

Limit options. There's such a thing as choice overload. In a key study on student choice, researchers Sheena Iyengar and Mark Lepper (2000) offered college students a short-essay assignment for extra credit. They gave one group a choice of six essay topics from which to choose. The second group was offered 30 choices. From the group with fewer choices, more of the students turned in the assignment. They also wrote better essays than those in the group with 30 choices. In this and other studies about student choice, Iyengar and Lepper concluded that excessive choices initially excited the choosers, but "undermined choosers' subsequent satisfaction and motivation" and left them "dissatisfied and having more regret about the choices they had made" (p. 1003). Offer students a moderate number of options from which to choose. Too many choices demotivate students!

Give choice about choices. In so many cases, students are capable of creating or helping to create the options for how to learn, how to show what they learn, how to evaluate their progress or performance, or how to set procedures for the classroom. Include students in brainstorming and deciding the options as often as possible.

Give feedback on choices. Provide feedback on students' choices—during and after the assignment or other situation in which they are acting on their choices. Give precise information and advice about what you see happening, how they've progressed, what you see them learning, what they might need to rethink, what they can improve, and what's working.

Teach students to monitor their progress. Before students begin assignments they've chosen, give them ways to evaluate their progress toward chosen goals. This can be in the form of rubrics, checklists, timelines, journals, or brief notes. They can stop at intervals and self-assess what they have learned or accomplished, asking themselves if there is anything they need to adjust or do differently or if there are any areas in which they need guidance. Even when the teacher offers the choices, look for situations in which the student can create his or her own (appropriate) option.

Don't consider choice an "add-on." Student choice is not something you add on to learning. It is not "supplemental" or "enrichment." It is something that should be an integral, required, normal part of everyday learning and classroom life. Benefits of student choice are not realized by one experience of choice. The benefits accrue as students have ongoing experiences making and following through with meaningful choices.

> Student choice is not something you add on to learning. It is not "supplemental" or "enrichment."

Beware of Grecian urns. Be careful not to sacrifice educational value in the name of giving students a choice. Many times students choose a "project" that turns out to be a choice with a "wow" factor, but one that doesn't really meet the educational goal. In her article "Is Your Lesson a Grecian Urn?" Jennifer Gonzalez (2016) argued that there are "far too many 'Grecian urns': projects that look creative, that the teacher might describe as hands-on learning, interdisciplinary teaching, project-based instruction, or the integration of arts or technology—but that nonetheless lack any substantial learning for students" (para. 7). She observed students making papier-mâché Grecian urns to meet a standard about understanding the complexity of a culture by exploring cultural elements. But when she talked to the students, it was clear that they had gained little or no understanding of the complexity of the ancient Greek culture. Yes, the students could choose how to design their urns. But the choice didn't lead them to the identified goal. (If the goal or standard had been in the field of visual arts, this might be a different story.)

Gonzalez encouraged teachers to consider each project: "Does it consume far more of a student's time than is reasonable in relation to its academic impact? If students spend more time on work that will not move them forward in the skill you think you are teaching, then it may be a Grecian urn. And it may need to go" (para. 17). She suggested that teachers can spot "Grecian urns" by watching out for excessive coloring or crafting, excessive "neat-o" tech, low-level thinking, a significant part of the grade being based on attractiveness or creativity, and word searches. Read her full article for advice on how to revise assignments that may be "Grecian urns" or "Grecian urn-ish." And remember the caution stated above: match the complexity of the choices to the complexity of the standard.

Examining a "Choice" Assignment

Here's how a teacher in Montana put student choice into practice. Her primary goal was to teach her sixth graders to *become* critical readers able to analyze and evaluate a text's purpose and ideas and the author's presentation of them. In this assignment, she also hoped to inspire students to appreciate literary texts and fall in love with reading by finding texts that connected to their lives and experiences. She said, "It's not just the content; it's the process. A student needs to be able to apply the process (and passion) to other works so that, with any text chosen, he can *become* a critical reader of that work."

To help students reach the goals (which include numerous English Language Arts standards), the teacher developed a reading model involving a good deal of choice. Early in the school year, students were given a list of different literary genres from which to choose reading selections. The requirement was to choose eight different literary works over the year from among nine different genres: traditional fiction, realistic fiction, historical fiction, science fiction, fantasy, mystery, biography, informational, and poetry. As the year went along, students chose works that matched their personal interests and curiosities. The teacher worked with students to ensure that their choices matched the chosen genre (i.e., *The Devil's Arithmetic* is not science fiction) and that they chose books appropriate for their individual reading abilities (high level readers shouldn't be choosing *The Three Little Pigs*, and readers struggling with sixth-grade level materials probably shouldn't be reading the seven novels in the *Harry Potter* series). Each student had the responsibilities of choosing wisely and completing the chosen books (and accompanying assignments).

Since the key academic goal had to do with critical reading skills, the teacher had prepared reading guides and assignments for each genre that students followed and completed as they read. In addition, she made a list of critical reading skills and compiled some questions that would lead students to develop abilities to understand each text and how the author wrote it. The list included such skills as previewing, identifying, and interpreting key purposes and messages of the text; describing tone; recognizing bias; making inferences; finding meaning; analyzing the author's storytelling and writing techniques; analyzing author techniques for developing characters; analyzing how a plot or main idea developed; analyzing parts of the text and how they relate to each other; and evaluating how (and how well) the author accomplished the purpose. Students used these lists to guide their reading; in addition, students conferred once a week with an adult. (Adults available for this included the teacher, a classroom paraprofessional, a parent volunteer, and another school staff member.) In the conference, the adult and student used the skills list and questions to work together toward mastering standards related to critical reading.

The teacher also offered students choices for how to demonstrate their progress toward *becoming* critical readers. They were required to choose a different option for each of the eight books they read. Some of the options were comparing the work to lyrics in multiple songs, writing and sharing a poem using similar techniques found in the poem they read, creating a comic strip to show development of a main idea, making a poster diagram to show relationships between ideas or events in the text, designing a "bias detector" slide show to share text evidence (illustrated) that revealed author bias, and writing a letter to the author critiquing the way the author accomplished her or his purpose.

Nothing increases the sense of *belonging* or *becoming* (in many different ways) as having the power, the say, the importance, the responsibility, the brain-stretching, the maturity, and the accomplishment that comes from sharing your voice, knowing your voice is wanted and respected, and having, exercising, and being accountable for your choices. Students want to know, "Do I see myself on the walls of the school?" "Am I in the eyes and hearts of the people who work with me at the school?" "Am I embraced as me—both the me I am now and the me I can *become?*" Giving students plenty of appropriate and meaningful choices and other opportunities to elevate their voices allows each one to answer "Yes!" to all these questions.

Putting It into Practice

As an individual, team, small group, or entire staff, use some of these activities to spark discussions, reflect on your current practices or situations, listen to others, or set goals.

1. Review the data your school collects to reflect on improvement. Does it include students' perceptions? If so, are these perceptions gathered informally from staff or from surveys of students? Are the perceptions from a school-wide or classroom perspective? Discuss how your school uses these data to help with continuous improvement. Do you report back to students about steps taken for improvement based on their perceptions? If you don't seek out students' perceptions, what can you do to change that?

2. Ask teachers to bring at least one example of the best instructional strategy used to give students choice in their classrooms. Create sharing groups by mixing teachers across subject areas, teams, and grade levels. Have each group choose a recorder to list ideas and the name of the teacher who shared it. Collect the lists from all groups, compile the ideas, and share them with everyone.

3. Ask staff members to respond to questions similar to the following, "What would students say if asked . . ."
   — How often do classroom assignments allow for choice for students?
   — What opportunities do students have to share their ideas and concerns?
   — Are student concerns listened to and acted upon? Why or why not?
   — What kinds of choices can students make in how they learn something, how they show what they learn, and how that learning is assessed?
   — Do you have assignments that lean toward being "Grecian urns"? How can you improve the educational value of these assignments?

   Then convene a group of students and ask them the same questions. Share student answers with the staff, and then compare and contrast answers. Were there surprises? Given the answers, identify areas that need work, change, or improvement.

Chapter 8

Develop Student Leadership

"Education is too important to be left solely to educators."
- Francis Keppel

Middle school students! They want to be active. They want to participate in real life situations. Some want to serve. Some want to be in
charge. Some are curious about the world around them and want to
make it a better place; they can be very compassionate to those less
fortunate than themselves. All young adolescents have a strong need to
belong. And we can help them *become* more caring and compassionate
preteens, teens (and eventually, adults) who can help others and who
can help to make their schools and world better places.

Those of us who work with students "in the middle" recognize the
desire they have to contribute their energies and ideas to make a
difference. But we sometimes struggle with just how to help them
do that. When students take leadership roles, even small ones, they
belong to their schools and communities in new and meaningful ways.
Leadership also moves students along paths to *becoming* in many of

the ways we've already discussed in this book. Authentic leadership experiences draw on and accelerate growth in such qualities as self-motivation, self-efficacy, confidence, self-determination, self-discipline, healthy relationships, ethical development, confidence, autonomy, competence, communication, and expression of voice (Fletcher, 2003a, 2003b: Van Velsor & Wright, 2012; Mozhgan, Parivash, Nadergholi, & Jowkar, 2011).

The development of leadership skills and traits also has a direct impact on students' engagement and academic success in the classroom. Students tend to apply such leadership skills as organization, communication, time management, problem solving, courage to take risks, and collaborating effectively with others to complete tasks to improve their academic performances. These students often *become* role models for their peers and play an important part in helping create a positive school and classroom environment (Beaudin, 2005; Cook-Sather, 2002; Fielding, 2006).

Cementing the Foundations of Leadership Development

A six-year old neighbor of mine (Patti) told me she loves being the line leader in her kindergarten class. I asked her why (in truth, expecting that her reason would have to do with the good feeling of being first). Her answer: "I like being the one who gets to help everyone get to where they want to go." When a middle school orchestra performs its spring concert, my friend's son conducts one of the pieces. (Five other orchestra members each conduct a piece also). His self-esteem and confidence, along with his music skills, have soared. A niece, who is a high-school sophomore, mentors a group of sixth graders in an exploratory coding class. She's developing teaching skills and relationship skills; at the same time, she's stretching her own understanding of coding processes as she works to restate them in ways the younger students can understand.

The benefits of student leadership experiences—from short to long-term or simple to sophisticated—are countless. When schools provide opportunities for all students to gain and practice leadership skills, they offer exciting ways for all students to grow personally and academically. In addition, and also extremely important, student leadership is integral to the development of a positive, connected school community; **all members of the community benefit** when many students take on leadership roles (Matthews, 2015). Schools do a better job of accomplishing their missions and nurturing their students (and faculty) when students learn to lead. And the colleges, workplaces, governments, and other organizations in our society and world need capable leaders in the generations to come. Where will these leaders come from? They must come from our schools! "Leadership training for our students is an investment in our present and future" (Lewis, Hunter, & Green, 2009).

In 2012, the Center for Creative Leadership took an online survey of business, government, nonprofit, and education leaders to ask a series of questions about leadership needs and qualities. This *Leadership Insights Survey* included questions about the age at which students should begin leadership experiences, whether leadership development should be part of the regular school curriculum, and how widely leadership training should be offered. Of the 462 respondents from all sectors of the economy, 97% believed that leadership development should begin by age 21, with 90% saying before age 18 and 50% believing it should begin in elementary school. In addition, the report showed that "the vast majority of respondents (84%) believe leadership development opportunities should be offered to **all youth,** and an even higher number (90%) feel it should be a part of **every** student's educational experience" (Van Velsor & Wright, pp. 2-4).

Adam Fletcher (2013), creator of the Meaningful Student Involvement (MSI) model for school improvement, argues that students should be equal partners in all phases of the operation of a school. The MSI model "promotes student engagement by securing roles for students in every facet of the educational system and recognizes the unique knowledge, experience, and perspective of each individual student" (para. 1). Fletcher also states,

> Every day more educators are showing that they value students by involving them in meaningful ways in school. These teachers and administrators say that it is not about "making students happy" or allowing students to run the school. Their experience shows that when educators partner with students to improve learning, teaching and leadership in schools, school change is positive and effective (2003a, p. 4).

In 2003, Fletcher was hopeful as he saw more educators valuing greater student involvement in their schools. Yet, the researchers who carried out the 2012 *Leadership Insights Survey* reflected that, "despite the widespread agreement reflected in the results, leadership development for all and a part of **every student's educational experience** is clearly not happening in the lives of most youth today" (Van Velsor & Wright, p. 4).

The foundations for all student leadership efforts in our schools will come from what we believe about students and leadership. Just as with other programs that elevate development of crucial aspects of *belonging* and *becoming* for students, leadership development programs must start with examination and clarification of our beliefs and philosophies. Fortunately, beliefs related to this topic should flow naturally from commitments we have already made to create connected, caring communities; believe in students; promote their self-efficacy and autonomy; and champion student voice and choice.

Authors of *The Handbook for Student Leadership Development* (2011) include these in the beliefs they see as foundational to student leadership development:

- Leadership can be learned.
- Leadership is developmental.
- All students can develop leadership.

- All schools must find ways to develop leadership capabilities and skills for all students. (Komives, Dugan, Owen, Slack, & Wagner, p. xvi).

The staff in each school, ideally in collaboration with students and parents, can take a fresh look at the practices and programs for student leadership. We educators can ask what these practices show about our beliefs. When we examine our current beliefs and practices, we should look at all the facets of our school and all existing leadership development efforts. This needs to include the leadership development that naturally occurs for many students in classrooms, on sports teams, and in all the organized clubs and groups on our campuses. We should take the time to clarify the goals for any programs (formal or informal) we have and for any we wish to add. Our examination must include a close look at how we chose the goals, how we chose the activities and programs, and how the facets of our overall program are monitored and evaluated.

If we share the beliefs above, we certainly can't continue to see leadership development experiences primarily as exclusive clubs that include only certain students (Van Velsor & Wright, 2012). We can't rely primarily on sports teams and other extracurricular programs to provide the leadership experiences students need.

> **We can't rely primarily on sports teams and other extracurricular programs to provide the leadership experiences students need.**

We must expand the definition to new, creative, and diverse options that offer possibilities for all students to gain the benefits of leadership—leadership they experience for themselves and leadership they see in other students.

Rethinking Student Leadership Training

Schools are at different places in their efforts to address leadership development. The programs they design must fit the unique needs of their students. But when the belief and commitment are to include all students in meaningful ways, schools must strive to

1. Raise the level of leadership skills and qualities for all students.

2. Raise the level of student participation in leadership by giving students real opportunities with enough possibilities that allow them all to actually be leaders.

Developing Leadership Skills and Qualities

When we considered and researched the skills and qualities of leadership, we ended up with a long list. (When you consider this topic, you'll likely think of things to make it even longer!) Also, we quickly became aware of how much the composition of the list reminded us of the skills and qualities we've discussed throughout this book. But they take on new meaning and new urgency in the context of the leadership development that is so necessary and possible for our middle level students.

At first we were overwhelmed by the all-inclusiveness of the skills and attributes our students need to be leaders. This is true whether we think of student leadership in roles that seem large (ongoing or public, with lots of extensive contributions) or small (short-term, part of everyday school experiences). We thought, "How do we fit in a whole new repertoire of skills to teach?" We quickly realized that schools and teachers already take these skills and qualities seriously and that attention to them is already a part of school classrooms, programs, and practices. What we educators need to do now is think about how these skills and qualities relate to leadership roles and how to give students chances to develop them **within** leadership roles.

A good leader:
- Shows kindness and respect to all others.
- Speaks and acts responsibly.
- Inspires others to be better tomorrow and make some part of the world better.

- Is assertive but tactfully so.
- Is confident but not overbearing.
- Understands his or her strengths, challenges, and motivations.
- Values and welcomes all members of the community without any discrimination.
- Is eager to hear and embrace other viewpoints.
- Shares decision-making.
- Helps others feel confident.
- Makes other people better.
- Is humble.
- Is persistent.
- Keeps an open mind.
- Is creative; tries new approaches and ideas.
- Gives credit to others.
- Doesn't assume she or he knows the best way to do everything.
- Does not blame others but takes steps to do what he or she can to correct a situation.
- Focuses energy where it will do the most good.
- Expresses gratitude to others.
- Asks for and welcomes help.
- Communicates before acting.
- Consults with others.
- Takes initiative.
- Takes responsibility.
- Accepts and demonstrates accountability.
- Keeps a cool head.
- Works hard.
- Delegates; doesn't try to do everything alone.
- Models ethical behavior.
- Learns to deal with and respond to mistakes.

- Is willing to correct mistakes and learn from them.
- Shows passion about his or her beliefs.
- Has a sense of humor.
- Doesn't hog the spotlight; shines it on other people.
- Is truthful.
- Is trustworthy.
- Does not gossip.
- Invites evaluation of her or his leadership.
- Seeks to learn from others.
- Seeks to keep on learning.
- Uses personal power responsibly and caringly.
- Is real; says what he or she believes and is not trying to be somebody else.

Some leadership skills and qualities to develop, expand, and practice:

- Kindness
- Compassion
- Respect
- Effective speaking
- Respectful listening
- Self-expression
- Self-awareness
- Self-direction
- Making decisions
- Sharing decision-making
- Discussion
- Collaboration
- Conflict resolution
- Conflict response
- Goal setting
- Analyzing options and situations
- Reflection
- Giving and receiving feedback
- Flexibility
- Cultural awareness
- Building healthy relationships
- Emotional stability
- Emotional intelligence
- Responsibility
- Empathy
- Honesty
- Humility
- Courage
- Integrity
- Reasoning
- Reasoned, compassionate evaluation
- Self-esteem

- Self-belief
- Self-confidence
- Ethical behavior
- Organization and planning
- Problem solving

- Creating and making presentations
- Public speaking
- Project management
- Team building
- Working with a team

Development of these qualities and skills can be a part of every classroom and school activity. If they do not already, teachers can plan specific, targeted situations for students to make and defend decisions, identify and take different roles in classroom activities, practice giving and receiving feedback, analyze what they've learned, evaluate results of learning activities, discuss concerns in the classroom, learn from mistakes, solve conflicts, adapt plans due to changing circumstances, listen respectfully to one another, work in collaborative groups, write mission statements for a class or team, set goals and work to achieve them, design and carry out service projects, reflect on personal responses to classroom situations or group work, or to further any other quality or skill listed above.

Offering Plenty of Real Leadership Opportunities

To make strides toward leadership development for all students, educators must think creatively—beyond formal leadership programs. Yes, a fair number of students in a middle school can develop leadership in traditional clubs, sports teams, student councils, and leadership electives. But in most schools, that covers a relatively small number of students. And often schools do not intentionally specify, track, or evaluate what leadership skills actually are being developed within those programs or for which students. (A student can be on a sports team for years without developing or practicing leadership skills. She might see a good leader (the coach) in action, but she may not have chances to be a leader herself.)

The concept of offering leadership development for all students goes far beyond the idea of teaching all students a number of leadership skills—that is, teaching in a way that has students listening, watching, reading about, or discussing qualities and skills (but not actually doing any leading). It even goes beyond practicing those skills in real-life situations. While such learning is a necessary component, leadership lessons are more valuable, and more likely to be internalized, in experiential settings where the learner is **practicing leadership** (Matthews, 2015; Rosch & Meixner, 2011).

Schools must intentionally design situations in which each student has the experience of being the leader. This must be a school-wide approach based on school-wide goals. To meet the goal of reaching all students, most schools will need to add opportunities for experiences that hand leadership to students—within the regular curriculum, in their classrooms, in specialized leadership classes, in all school organizations, in partnerships outside the school, in service learning, and in community engagement. And because students are diverse, the school's plan must include diverse strategies and approaches (Komives, Dugan, Owen, Slack, & Wagner, 2011, p. xvi).

Adam Fletcher (2003a) describes conditions for "meaningful student involvement" (MSI, as his school improvement model calls it):

- Students develop complex learning skills.
- Students are equal partners in education.
- There is no discrimination regarding who can participate.
- Students are integrated into organizational and attitudinal change.
- Students gain validation through action and involvement that empowers them.
- Student participation in experiences is measurable and effective (pp. 10-11).

If students are to be equal partners, if they are to gain validation through powerful action and involvement, if all students can lead and should have chances to do so—and if we believe in student voice and choice—then we will certainly include students in planning leadership opportunities. And if we believe that there should be no discrimination regarding who can be leaders, and that a diverse student body (and all student bodies are diverse) means we must offer diverse approaches, then it's even more certain that students must take part planning the goals and details of a leadership development program that will interest them. That's the best way to ensure student enthusiasm, ownership, and engagement; it's the best way to ensure program success, as well.

Combining Possibilities Into Programs

An overall school design for student leadership development will likely be unique to the school itself. Cookie cutter programs are not as effective as those created to fit the needs of the students and the vision of the school (Lewis, Hunter, & Green, 2009). The specific program structure is not what matters. What matters is that it meets the conditions for meaningful student involvement and reaches the school's goals for leadership development for all students. Each school must ask how to increase authentic leadership experiences through which all of its students have many chances to be leaders.

As middle level leaders ourselves, we are enthusiastic about the rethinking of student leadership development. We're thrilled to witness what happens in the lives and enthusiasm of students (and their teachers and schools) when we expand the boundaries to offer all kinds of new leadership experiences for students. We encourage you to push the boundaries, too, to mix all kinds of options and to shape an overall student leadership development program that works for you, even if its shape is like none you've ever seen!

Top 6 Suggestions for Student Leadership Development

- Include all students in your plan to develop leadership skills.

- See that every student has several leadership experiences each week.

- Involve all students in leadership that serves others.

- Make relationships and ethics central to leadership training.

- Give students tools and time to reflect on leaders (including themselves).

- Intentionally plan ways to evaluate all components of your leadership development program.

Formalized Programs

Most schools have some formalized "leadership" experiences designed to build and promote leadership. Even these experiences need to be personalized to the needs of the specific school. Traditionally, leadership classes include leadership training. Other formalized programs, such as student councils—elected or appointed—probably include discussion and decision-making related to student concerns. But actual comprehensive leadership training may or may not be part of the experience. Students taking part in formalized experiences, whether they are elected, teacher-chosen, or volunteers, need to understand how their involvement and leadership impacts others (both positively and, if used inappropriately, possibly negatively). In a world that tends to be very self-centered (particularly at this age), a student needs to see how she, as one individual, can make a meaningful difference in someone else's life.

In the process of creating an overall plan for student leadership development, school staff (again, hopefully with student participation) need to consider the following for each formalized experience now in place or being considered: how it fits into the overall school goals and plan for leadership development, what leadership skills will be taught (and how and by whom), what responsibilities and activities the organization or experience will take on, how to involve as many students as possible, when and where it will take place, who will oversee it, and how it will be evaluated. Here are a few models being used in successful middle school programs around the country:

Elective or Exploratory Classes—Many schools run an effective leadership development program through their elective or exploratory program. In some cases students choose a leadership class or are assigned to it as a part of the schools' rotating cycle of electives. These classes may last a trimester or quarter to include as many students as possible in the experience. Depending on the school, a leadership class may be taught by an administrator, teacher, or counselor. (Schools might consider using a student as a co-leader, one who has completed the class and gained real leadership experience).

Voluntary Training—In some situations, schools run successful leadership programs simply by allowing as many students as want to attend (or can be handled by the leaders). For example, in one school we have visited, three leaders host a leadership class every Wednesday morning before school at 7:30. The only requirement is to be there on time. The classes have an average attendance of 90 students a week, with about 200 different students attending over the course of a year (and most of the 500 students at this school are bus riders).

Elected Leadership Groups—Many middle level schools use an elected student council model, while others have adapted this model so as to involve more students in leadership. Small groups of students may run for an office or position instead of an individual. Another variation on this model is to have each team choose two or three representatives to attend a weekly leadership meeting at the school. Each quarter, different students may be selected to attend.

Teacher-Selected Leadership Groups—In another model for student leadership organizations, staff members choose student leaders (students who obviously function as leaders—though their leadership may range from positive to not so positive). The goal is to guide students' leadership potential from wherever they are starting! This method also helps to curtail popularity contests for elections. Because this type of leadership group would limit those who participate, it is important that this not be the only leadership group on campus. (See the article titled "Student Leadership Council" (Appendix D) on pages 237–238 for more on this idea.)

Possibilities Beyond a "Program"

There are dozens of possibilities for experiential leadership learning opportunities—in the classroom and around the school—that can occur frequently and for many students beyond what we usually think of as "a program." These include such opportunities as

- Student-led decision-making groups within regular curriculum areas.
- Student-led cooperative learning groups.
- Student-planned and student-led lessons within the classroom.
- Student-planned and student-led classroom management processes.
- Peer tutoring.
- Peer mentoring.
- Mentoring or tutoring of students from younger grades.
- Student-led classroom or team meetings.
- Student-led conferences with the teacher.
- Student-led conferences with the principal.
- Student-led committees to make recommendations on a specific issue.
- Student-led task forces to research topics of concern.

In addition, a school can establish any number of leadership groups for a particular length of time or purpose. These can exist alongside the experiential lessons in classrooms and the established long-term leadership groups such as student councils and after-school programs. Below, we've described some activities that we have seen middle school student leadership groups plan and implement successfully. With any experiences such as these, make sure that students are taking the lead in planning, implementing, and evaluating.

Service in the Wider Community

- Host a back-to-school night for senior citizens. Have a school bus pick up residents from local retirement homes. Plan activities such as bingo, digital communication skills (tablets, computers, Internet use), dancing (it warms the heart to see a middle schooler jitterbugging with a senior citizen), a cakewalk, crafts, and more.

- Hold a "scavenger hunt" food drive for the needy. Students (and staff) form teams of eight, give themselves a name, and collect items on a list. Each item brought from the list (generally food or money) is worth a set number of points. Teams compete with each other to see who can accumulate the most points. The winning team is given a "night on the town" (i.e., pizza, movie coupons, bowling, etc.) Leadership kids plan and host a breakfast or lunch for the winning staff team.

- Adopt a local senior citizens residence or nursing home. Go Christmas caroling, plan a party for them, organize an old fashioned sing-along, take them cookies, or just go visit to get better acquainted.

- Participate in community events. Help out with Special Olympics or a Down's Syndrome Buddy Walk. Sponsor a booth at a local festival. Build a float for a holiday parade. Help put together food baskets at the local food bank. Ring the bell at holiday time for the Salvation Army.

- Partner with a local community service organization such as Rotary or the Lions Club to work together to meet the needs of the community (where oftentimes students and their families are the recipients of this community service).

School Climate Builders

- Leadership students can plan and host fun assemblies based on game shows (try "Family Feud" or "Who Wants to be a Millionaire?"), talent shows (variations of "America's Got Talent" or "The Voice," or athletic competitions (staff and students competing on tiny tricycles, running an obstacle course, etc.). Assemblies can also serve to introduce staff to students at the beginning of the year or to teach students the rules in a fun way (a dress code demonstration with teachers breaking the rules is always a big hit with students!).

- Recognize and celebrate staff. Students create a silly costume from the costume closet and visit staff members on their birthday; a song is sung, and birthday treats are served on a fancy tray. Give ornaments at holiday time. Bring treats for Teacher Appreciation Day. Host a brunch for secretary's week. Plan a special day to honor the custodial staff, office staff, kitchen staff, or maintenance staff, etc.

- Organize spirit days (everyone wears school colors), theme days (the 50s), holiday events (decorate doors for holidays), or contests (how many hearts in the glass display case).

- Produce a video to encourage proper behavior. Act out harassment situations. Have the narrator ask the viewers to stop the tape for a discussion. Finish by acting out several solutions.

- Invite members of the community to attend an assembly to take part in the "Hands are Not for Hurting" program. Visitors cut out their purple hands and take the pledge in front of the school. All students are then encouraged to make the pledge during the following days.

- Name (Student) of the Day. Each morning draw a student's name from a can and announce them as the name of the day. The winner comes to the office to receive a treat and other affirmations that the student group plans.

Service in the School

- Form a greeter's group to welcome new students, help them find their way around the school and learn school routines, sit with them at lunch (an important need for students), and help them navigate school life.

- Lobby to change school policies. (One group successfully lobbied the entire staff to change a long standing "no gum" policy.)

- Organize an activity night. Think beyond just a dance; show videos, have carnival type booths (face painting, bean bag toss), play games in the gym, compete at bingo, have a karaoke contest, etc.

- Be responsible for changing the school reader board, running the school recycling program, or reading the morning announcements over the intercom.

- Help with fifth grade orientation and fall registration. Be tour guides for school visitors.

- Organize a skate night for students and parents from the entire school district or your feeder elementary schools.

- Host a "transition to high school" event for eighth graders. Bring in high school students and staff to share experiences and information.

Fundraisers

- Hold a penny war. Create containers for each grade level as well as one for the staff. A penny placed in a container gives that group one point. Silver or paper money counts for negative points (a dime is -10, a dollar bill -100). Students try to put pennies in their team's jar and silver or paper money in the other teams' jars.

- Sell hat passes. If your school has a no hats rule, on a given day let students purchase a hat pass to wear on a special "Hats On" Day. Students who purchase a button with an anti-drug message (or for some other cause) may wear a hat as long as the button is showing.

- Students donate money to get a staff member (or a group of staff members) to do something embarrassing (like kissing a pig or getting a pie in the face) in front of the entire school.

- Hold a car wash. Take pledges for a Bowl-a-thon or Jog-a-thon. Have a bottle drive.

Earlier in the book we emphasized the part that teacher-student relationships play in helping students to *belong* to their classrooms and school and to *become* in a multiplicity of areas of growth. Leadership development is yet another area of *belonging* and *becoming* where relationships play a key role. Middle school students often erect smokescreens that make it hard to identify their potential or interests. But a teacher, advisor, or other adult advocate who has gotten to know the individual student and has a built a trusting relationship with him or her knows the student's talents and interests. This is the very person who can steer the student toward fitting leadership opportunities and support him or her in the development of leadership. In the presence of a strong adult-student relationship, there is a valuable resource to identify student potential—and to connect that student with other students who share the same interests and potential. This can help to increase the sense of *belonging* at the same time the student is *becoming* a leader!

I (Patti) remember a student in my middle school in southern Oregon where such a relationship paid off to help a student who otherwise might never have found her way into any positive leadership situation. The school established a peer mediation program—a form of conflict resolution that trained students to help their peers work together to resolve everyday disputes. For such a program to work effectively, it's important to select peer mediators who mirror the population of the school. A teacher recommended a student for the program who, at first chance, appeared to be a poor choice. Julia was a bully, known for disruptive behavior; yet she was "popular" with a large number of students—possibly because they admired her "power." But the teacher knew more about Julia than the rest of us, and he had faith in Julia's potential. Trusting the teacher's advice and relationship with Julia, we took a risk. We selected Julia for the program. She participated fully and attended all the training (that involved mentoring in skills of leadership, collaboration, and conflict resolution, as well as skills of self-regulation, interpersonal relationships, and respect). Julia became one of the most effective mediators we ever had in the program. By the next year, she had turned herself around to become a positive force in the school. She continued with the program into high school and eventually became a speaker and representative for the organization that provided the initial training. This all happened because a teacher who had built a relationship with her recognized Julia's potential even as most of the rest of us saw her as troublesome.

Other Thoughts and Advice on Leadership Development

- Every quarter, when you review assessments and progress for all other areas of *belonging* and *becoming*, create a category for examining each student's participation in leadership development training and experiences. Create a checklist or table where you can keep track of all the chances each individual has been given for authentic leadership.

- Every student leadership group needs an adult guide who has a heart for kids and for the mission of the group. This is a must!

- Communicate leadership events regularly and clearly with the remainder of the staff and students.

- During and after leadership activities, review and stress concepts and qualities of leadership.

- Emphasize responsibility and accountability throughout all leadership experiences for students.

- Use lots of hand-on and team-building activities, but don't forget to add a reflective component.

- Have a focal point for your fundraising activities. Adopt a pet project. For example, in Oregon many student leadership groups joined the effort to raise money to build a new state children's hospital. The end result? The young people raised over a million dollars!

- Think beyond using just teachers or administrators as advisors or overseers to student leadership groups. Two classified employees and one teacher started an outstanding leadership program at one of our schools.

- Just because students are in a leadership group does not mean they will be actual leaders. You have to make this happen. When such a group plans events, the adult supervisor should not be the leader with a student as an assistant. Students must be the leaders or co-leaders for events. Rotate student leadership so that large numbers of students have experience in leader roles.

- Students need to explore traits of effective leaders. Students can shadow the mayor of their town, attend a school board meeting, or design and administer a survey for local leaders to answer (including high school student leaders and team captains).

- Students need experiences reflecting on leaders and leadership. Once students learn some qualities of good leaders, they should reflect on what they see in leaders around them—in their school, community, state, nation, and in the world. Ask them to think about their role models and celebrities as leaders and make evaluations about them as leaders.

- One of the most important roles for leaders and leadership groups is to serve others. See that all students have experiences in using their leadership skills to help someone else.

A newspaper in Lynchburg, Virginia, featured a story about a middle school leadership skills class developed by seventh-grade science teacher Moose Pierce. One of the valuable lessons students learned in this class, the reporter observed, was that leaders make things better for others. We'd like to end our chapter on student leadership development with the teacher's parting words at the end of the class. They leave us (and students) with a message that should be a central theme of any student leadership development program; they speak to a prime example of what we want our students to *become*. Before he dismissed the class, Pierce gave this homework assignment to his students: "Ladies and gentlemen, please look for an opportunity to do good" (Pounds, 2014).

Putting It into Practice

As an individual, team, small group, or entire staff, use some of these activities to spark discussions, reflect on your current practices or situations, listen to others, or set goals.

1. Make a list of leadership opportunities available to students at your school. Review the list and determine how many of the activities involve organizing activities (school dance, can food drive, etc.) versus leading (principal advisory group, making changes to school procedures, peer mediation, mentoring, etc.). Is the balance between organizing versus leading appropriate? Are you too heavy on one side? What types of opportunities are missing?

2. Examine your school's data on student leadership. How many students are given the opportunity to participate in leadership development—in formalized or "casual" programs? Do the formalized programs involve groups that are heterogeneously mixed (in gender, "social" group, age, socioeconomic status, ethnicity, etc.)? How can you use these data to improve opportunities for more students?

3. Work with students to create a survey on student leadership in your school. Let the students inform you about what students perceive about leadership development, whether they are actually having leadership experiences, what student leadership contributes to their school lives, and what changes they would suggest. Be sure students are involved in reviewing, analyzing, and reporting the results. Be sure that school governing and decision-making bodies listen to what students have to say about this topic.

Chapter 9

Celebrate Belonging and Becoming

"Celebrate what you want to see more of."

- Tom Peters

Acknowledging what students do right can never be wrong! Too often in education, there is a focus on what needs to be fixed, on what needs to improve. So much energy is poured into addressing problems students have (or create) that there's little energy left to pay attention to what's working, growing, or going well. In this book, we've framed the mission and goals of middle level education in terms of students' *belonging* and *becoming*. If these processes (and the dozens of qualities, behaviors, and skills that they entail) are what our work with middle level students is all about, then *belonging* and *becoming* are what all students and educators need to celebrate!

When we use the phrase "what students do right," we mean to expand the "do right" idea far beyond the boundaries of playing by all the rules, achieving diligently, or being model students. There are hundreds of ways students can do something right (something that shows their growth in *belonging* or *becoming*). Within each student there are many actions, behaviors, and accomplishments to recognize and celebrate—if we educators are there to notice, if we enlist students in looking for them, and if we expand what we are looking for.

The very process of learning to celebrate enhances students' *belonging* and *becoming*. When they recognize what they have contributed, their *belonging* increases. When they recognize what they have accomplished, their awareness of *becoming* increases. When they celebrate with a group of students, they gain affirmation that increases *belonging* and boosts *becoming* for all of them. Researchers Alan Hoffman and Sharon Field found that self-determination increased when students learned to reflect on experiences and to celebrate successes (Hoffman & Field, 1995). As students examine and acknowledge their own growth, they make strides toward *becoming* as learners and thinkers.

When there is an intentional plan to look for, notice, appreciate, and celebrate students' growth in positive directions—it's good for everyone in the school. We all know that teachers and administrators can't ignore the reality of changing classes, pretend lunch with 300 adolescents isn't happening, or act as if the bus loading zone doesn't exist. A parent isn't likely to call the school to complain, "You didn't brag on my child today." Yet that same parent will most certainly call if his child feels unsafe in the halls because there isn't enough adult supervision during class changes, doesn't get to eat lunch, or misses the bus home. We tend to address the things we have to do and ignore the things that are not urgent or required. But when we change our thinking and see celebrating students as equally urgent and required to class change, lunch duty, and bus dismissal, adults benefit,

> **When there is an intentional plan to look for, notice, appreciate, and celebrate students' growth in positive directions—it's good for everyone in the school.**

too. You'll be amazed at the positive impact on the entire school culture and the attitudes of teachers, administrators, and all staff members. When students' growth is celebrated, so is the work of the adults who helped them belong and become.

Deciding What to Celebrate

Back in Chapter 1, we described many characteristics to form a definition and picture of both *belonging* and *becoming*. At the end of the chapter, we encouraged you to create your own lists of what is included in *belonging* and *becoming* in your school and classrooms. In the Conclusion (see pages 213–225), you'll find middle level students' reflections on manifestations of *belonging* and actions that help students *belong*. Let these lists and reflections be your guidelines when you consider what to celebrate!

For example, if you see that your students *belong* to their school when they . . .

- Feel a sense of identification with their school or groups in it.
- Feel safe at school—both physically and psychologically.
- Feel that they have a voice in school.
- Feel respected throughout the school.
- Believe in their own indispensability to the group.
- Trust their teachers and their peers.
- Believe that they have as much value as anyone else.
- Are confident that others see them as valuable.
- Feel securely connected with others in their school and classes.
- See themselves as being part of a supportive community.
- Not only feel support but also are able to accept it.
- Feel wanted and needed.
- Feel like individuals, not stereotypes.
- Perceive and trust that the *belongingness* they feel is likely to continue.

... then these are the things to look for and celebrate when you see them! When students visibly show signs of *belonging*, when they reflect on their sense of *belonging* and can tell how and why it is there or has grown, when they can describe their personal *belonging* in positive terms—**celebrate**! When you, or students, or anyone else in the school sees a student **do** something to help another student *belong*—recognize and affirm this.

Likewise, if you believe that your students are *becoming* when they ...

- Learn academic skills and processes and show their learning proficiently.
- Hone various processes for continued learning.
- Build a necessary base of knowledge.
- Think critically.
- Learn to find, process, evaluate, and use information.
- Take on challenges, reaching beyond what they thought they could do.
- Strive for mastery.
- Work productively within groups.
- Engage effectively in discussions.
- Reflect on and process their own learning and behaviors.
- Make reasoned evaluations about real-life situations and influences.
- Contribute to the well-being of the school community.
- Explore new ideas and interests.
- Make responsible choices and decisions.
- Grow in autonomy.
- Take risks; try new ideas.
- Express their voices.
- Interact with others in healthy ways.
- Show curiosity and inventiveness.
- Demonstrate persistence.
- Recover from failure, disappointment.

- Learn from correcting mistakes.
- Develop a growth mindset.
- Expand learning beyond their community.
- Develop skills to learn and interact with others.
- Use technology proficiently, ethically, and safely.
- Set and work to achieve goals.
- Participate productively in their society.
- Dream big and seek to discover what their futures may hold.
- Demonstrate respect for and acceptance of all people around them.
- Show compassion.
- Resolve conflicts.
- Develop hopeful, optimistic attitudes toward learning and life.
- Solve problems of all kinds independently and with others.
- Regulate their behaviors.
- Cope with peer pressure.
- Channel emotions in positive ways.
- Deal positively with stress.
- Believe in themselves.
- Persist to finish a task or reach a goal.
- Develop resilience.
- Take on leadership roles.
- And show any number of other behaviors or qualities on your *becoming* and *belonging* list . . .

. . . then these are the things to look for and **celebrate** when you see them! It's an occasion to celebrate whenever we see students actively trying, making progress at, or mastering any of academic or personal qualities, skills, or behaviors of *becoming*. Watch for them in students. Have students watch for them in each other. Model them yourself; this is cause for celebration. Recognize and affirm them as often as possible.

In addition, let's celebrate each other. Teachers, administrators, and students can notice examples of our efforts to

- Develop trusting, caring teacher-student, student-student, and adult-adult relationships.
- Offer learning experiences that are engaging and relevant.
- Give students second (and third and fourth) chances to succeed.
- Work together to move everyone toward a growth mindset.
- Do a better school-wide job of enhancing student voice and choice.
- Build a connected school community.

Considering How to Recognize and Reward

Teachers and other adults in the school recognize and affirm students dozens of times in many ways every day. There are frequent verbal encouragements; adults constantly seek to boost self-confidence, acknowledge hard work, and affirm learning of new skills and reaching new goals. The process of encouraging academic and personal growth and acknowledging when we see it happen often includes rewards and incentives. Many schools have school-wide programs to encourage and reward positive behavior.

Rethinking Recognitions and Rewards

A growing swell of research in the field of motivation has taken a hard look at how rewards, particularly extrinsic awards and incentives, affect students' behavior. A major conclusion of this research is that outside rewards often undermine students' intrinsic motivation. This has given us pause to reconsider many of the ideas we had about "motivating" students. There's no question that young children have self-motivation. Just watch a preschooler try to climb a ladder or get dressed by herself. Kids start out curious, constantly exploring and discovering, trying to do things for themselves. But often, somewhere along the way, many young people learn that they can "get something" for doing what they are supposed to do. Often that "something" is a tangible reward; often that "something" is approval from an adult.

Albert Bandura (1997) found self-efficacy to be foundational to motivation. The roots of self-motivation, he claimed, lie in one's belief that she has power over her own life and can effect changes in her life—in essence, that she is able to create satisfaction or success for herself. Bandura's research found that the higher a sense of self-efficacy a person has, the greater will be the intrinsic motivation, the harder he will work toward a goal, and the longer he will persist. Bandura also found that persons with higher self-efficacy were able to recover more quickly from failure.

> **The roots of self-motivation lie in one's belief that she has power over her own life and can effect changes in her life.**

Other researchers (Deci, Koestner, & Ryan, 2001) explored the conditions for fostering self-motivation and found that students learn best when they go after challenges of their own volition. Their intrinsic motivation leads to greater learning and greater satisfaction with learning, while extrinsic rewards dampen self-motivation, particularly the motivation to perform tasks individuals choose or tasks that are highly interesting to them. The results of a meta-analyses of well-controlled experiments exploring the effects of extrinsic rewards on intrinsic motivation showed that "all tangible rewards, all expected rewards, engagement-contingent rewards, completion-contingent rewards, task-contingent rewards, and performance-contingent rewards significantly undermined intrinsic motivation" (p. 14).

Extrinsic rewards can lead to behaviors that are the exact opposite of what we'd hoped to encourage. In an often-cited study on rewards, researchers gave children tangible rewards for drawing more often.

But when the reward was removed, the students drew less often than they had before and were less likely to draw later for pleasure (Letter, Greene, & Nisbett, 1973). Other studies led to similar conclusions: a reward may initially motivate the student, but after a while it can cause a loss of interest, diminish intrinsic motivation, and sometimes extinguish the behavior all together (Deci 1995; Deci, Koestner, & Ryan, 2001; Ryan & Deci 2000a; Kohn, 1993, 2001).

In his book *Drive: The Surprising Truth About What Motivates Us* (2011), Daniel Pink summarizes the flaws of "carrots and sticks" (a system of extrinsic rewards and punishments):

1. They can extinguish intrinsic motivation.

2. They can diminish performance.

3. They can crush creativity.

4. They can crowd out good behavior.

5. They can encourage cheating, shortcuts, and unethical behavior.

6. They can become addictive.

7. They can foster short-term thinking (p. 58).

Just about all educators praise students for hard work, meeting goals, or behaving appropriately (these are verbal rewards). We'd wager that the words "good job!" come out of the mouths of teachers and coaches more often than any other expression of affirmation. But even praise can be less effective, or perhaps even more harmful, than we've thought. Praise can become so generalized, repetitive, and automatic that it loses authenticity. "Good job!" "Well done!" "I'm so proud of you!" lose their meaning.

As with other forms of extrinsic rewards, praise can undermine intrinsic motivation. Students can become dependent on adult approval rather than find pride in themselves. Alfie Kohn (1993, 2001) says we've created "praise junkies" whose self-efficacy and self-motivation are harmed when the child works to accomplish something because it will please an adult. Kohn (2001) describes five problems with praise.

1. It can be manipulative—reinforcing something that is dependent on the adult's convenience or feelings.

2. It can create praise junkies, making children dependent on our evaluations about what is appropriate behavior.

3. It can steal the child's pleasure. "A child deserves to take delight in her accomplishments, to feel pride in what she's learned to do. She also deserves to decide when to feel that way" (para. 10).

4. It can cause children to lose interest in sustaining the behavior once the reward is over.

5. It can have the effect of reducing achievement. This is because praise puts pressure on the child, so he takes fewer risks and does more poorly than the students who weren't praised.

In an interview with James Morehead (2012) of OneDublin.com, Carol Dweck cautions us to take particular care not to praise students for their intelligence or ability. Praising students for being smart, she claims, backfires. "It puts them in a fixed mindset and not wanting challenges. They don't want to risk looking stupid or risk making mistakes. Kids praised for intelligence curtail their learning in order to never make a mistake, in order to preserve the label you gave to them" (2012).

Learning about how outside rewards (including verbal rewards) may affect students' own motivation does not suggest that we quit encouraging, complimenting, or celebrating their behaviors and accomplishments. It means, instead, that we do so thoughtfully—that we learn to do it in ways that

Intrinsic motivation flourishes in settings that encourage autonomy, competence, and relatedness.

are non-manipulative and that boost students' sense of control and their own joy in what they've done.

Intrinsic motivation flourishes in settings that encourage autonomy, competence, and relatedness (connection to the student's interests, personal goals, other schoolwork, and their lives outside school) (Deci, 1995; Deci & Ryan, 1985, 1987; Ryan & Deci, 2000a, 2000b; Dweck & Leggett, 1988; Assor, Kaplan, & Roth, 2002). Like self-motivation, self-efficacy is heightened when a student masters something challenging and experiences a new sense of competency (Bandura, 1997). In addition, tangible rewards do not have the same dampening effect on self-motivation if "they are not expected or not contingent on task behavior." In other words, when students don't feel controlled by the rewards, the use of them doesn't do the same damage to their self-efficacy and self-motivation (Deci, Koestner, & Ryan 1999, p. 653).

In her research on how rewards affect creativity, Teresa Amabile (1996) also found that an extrinsic reward can have a positive effect if it is given unexpectedly, as a congratulation. She recommends, as do others, that we not use extrinsic rewards as carrots, but, instead, give the reward when effort is obvious or a task is completed. In a report summarizing findings from studies on student motivation, the Center on Education Policy (2012) explains that rewarding specific actions that students can control—completing homework, mastering a specific task or skill, reading a book, or solving a tricky math problem—works better to motivate students than rewarding accomplishments that may seem beyond their reach or out of their control (p. 3).

Alfie Kohn (2001) suggests some alternatives to praise that support students' self-motivation rather than leading students to lean on adult approval. He encourages adults to consider saying nothing (let the child make his own decision about how the accomplishment makes him feel), stating what you saw (without evaluation, let her know you noticed), and asking questions (get him talking about his experience with and feelings about the accomplishment). Other research finds that verbal feedback does enhance intrinsic motivation when it is sincere, gives feedback on specific tasks, promotes autonomy, boosts self-efficacy, and helps to increase competence (Henderlong & Lepper, 2002).

Top 9 Tips for Celebrating Belonging and Becoming

- See that every student is authentically celebrated many times.

- Broaden the criteria for recognition to include many qualities and actions of belonging and becoming.

- Recognize input more often than output.

- Celebrate effort, not ability.

- Avoid rewards that make students dependent on adult approval.

- Use rewards in ways that boost student autonomy, competency, and relatedness.

- Teach students to celebrate with self-rewards.

- Celebrate the intangible rewards of belonging and becoming.

- Involve students in designing recognition programs and in choosing rewards.

Recognizing and Rewarding Thoughtfully

Of course we want to avoid recognition and rewards that diminish students' self-belief and self-motivation. We want to preserve their natural curiosity and interest, not dampen it. We want them to celebrate their accomplishments as coming from themselves. We want them to be proud of themselves. And we certainly don't want them to think they complete academic tasks, treat each other kindly, or make responsible choices to please an adult or get a slice of pizza. We don't want them to become addicted to getting a prize for something they should be doing anyway. Intrinsic motivation is part of *becoming* the best we can be—isn't this what we want for our students?

Most schools wrestle with the question of how to celebrate students' successes—and even how to define success. Already in this chapter, we've given you some suggestions about relating success to aspects of *belonging* and *becoming*. We honor the power of intrinsic motivation and believe that, ultimately, students have to find the will within themselves to achieve and prosper. At the same time, realistically, we see that extrinsic motivation has a role in what humans do. Think about the adults you know. Does Pete run because he loves running or because his doctor has told him he must lose weight? Does Cyndi drive at the speed limit because it's the safe thing to do or because she's afraid of getting a speeding ticket? Does Roberto clean his house because he loves to do housework, because he doesn't want to live in a dirty house, or because his wife will nag him if he doesn't help with housecleaning? Does Sue go to work because she thoroughly enjoys the work she does or because it pays a good salary? In many cases, our motivations are probably some combination of internal and external.

So what do we do?

- We remember that what we want for our students is to *belong* and *become*.

- We work at habits of thinking about what messages our words and acts of recognition give to students: Do they contribute to increased sense of being valuable, wanted, respected (*belonging*)? Do they state specific things that you've seen students trying, changing, working hard to complete (*becoming*)? Do they help the student feel more competent (*becoming*)? Do they encourage students to rely on their beliefs in themselves (*becoming*)? Do they help the student feel more powerful (*becoming*)? Are they tailored to the task and the student rather than clichéd (*becoming*)? And are they sincere?

- We cannot plan for rewards and recognition (celebrations) without coming to terms with what we believe about them. When we do use praise and other extrinsic rewards, we do so with a better understanding of how to be sure they work.

We plan to celebrate students in ways that bolster students' internal motivation, develop their autonomy, increase their competence, and relate to their lives.

- We pay close attention all day, every day to what we say and do—to be sure it gives the messages about rewards that we truly want to give.

Here are some guidelines to keep in mind as you use rewards (including verbal rewards), recognition, and rewards systems that let you delight in and celebrate with students as they seek to *belong* and *become*.

- Try to avoid using rewards as incentives—as something students know for sure they will "get" if they accomplish something specified. Reward at the end of a task without mentioning the reward at the beginning of the task.

- When you use extrinsic rewards, start with a reward as a motivational nudge, but reduce the frequency so as allow students to experience internal satisfaction for the behavior rather than depending on the reward.

- Use tangible rewards—trophies, certificates, prizes—judiciously and occasionally.

- Give recognition more often than tangible rewards.

- Recognize or reward such behaviors as competence, persistence, resilience, creativity.

- Recognize and reward things students can control—many small things in a day.

- Prize mastery of skills over final, absolute performance.

- Praise input more than output.

- Identify behaviors, rather than outcomes, to encourage.

- Recognize or reward progress toward goals or reaching a specific goal.

- Recognize or reward success that is within students' grasp.

- Adapt rewards to individuals. The same rewards don't work for all students.

- When giving recognition, describe what the student did or is doing ("You defended a claim with relevant, powerful information. Your argument convinced the entire audience!" "You stood up to the kids who were bullying Simone. That took courage, and it helped Simone feel safer.")

- Instead of statements about yourself ("Your attitude makes me feel good" or "This makes me proud of you," help them make statements that describe their own satisfaction or pride "You must be proud of yourself. How does it feel to have solved that problem?"

- Rewards work better and are more meaningful when students can choose something. Let them identify special privileges or activities that are appropriate rewards.

- Include rewards other than tangible prizes—things students like to do, such as extra recess time or technology time, time to collaborate with a group, time to read or write, time to listen to music, a dance-off, etc. (Try to include rewards that increase relationships and connections.)

- Help students understand the reasons for these desired behaviors—that they make school a healthy, growing place for everyone.

- Help students understand the meanings and value of their behaviors—how they connect to their well-being and their lives in and outside school.

- Ask students questions that help them reflect on their success experiences.

- Teach students how they can monitor and celebrate their own success.

- Teach students to self-reward—find ways to congratulate themselves for meeting goals.

- Find ways for students to (genuinely) affirm each other.

In some cases, the extrinsic rewards seem to be our best tool to motivate behavior that doesn't seem to change or develop any other way. Knowing well that the end goal is to foster self-motivation, sometimes we have to begin with the small steps of what might seem like blatant bribery. There are many times as a teacher or principal that I (Patti) used extrinsic rewards in small steps to help a student gain the experience of a healthy, safe, or productive behavior. But I recall one situation that challenged me profoundly to juggle the belief in intrinsic motivation with the usefulness of an extrinsic reward.

One late October, a student abruptly transferred into my sixth-grade classroom from another room in the school. I was never told the reason for the transfer; I only learned that the student was challenging and not doing well with the other teacher. "Challenging" was putting it mildly. Andrew was new to the school; he was taller and more physically developed than the other sixth graders. He could see shapes and shadows but was legally blind. He was a diabetic who needed insulin on a regular basis, bi-racial in a primarily white community, and spoke in a loud, deep voice. His verbal and physical actions intimidated other students; they were leery of becoming friends with him, and his overall behavior was disruptive to the learning.

Andrew's mother tried to be cooperative as I worked to help him to improve his social skills and focus better on his learning, but she was at her wit's end and didn't understand the issues; she claimed he was a "model" child at home. In her eagerness to help, she offered to come and sit in the back of the classroom every day so she could watch his actions. I discouraged that idea, explaining that her presence would likely cause Andrew to behave differently. A few days later, she arrived at the classroom door before students were admitted to the building. She was very excited about a plan she had devised that would allow her to sit in the back without Andrew knowing she was there. Her plan? She had already started on it—she was wearing a gorilla suit and carrying the head under her arm. (She intended to put it on when the students entered.) Needless to say, that plan was not put into practice.

I continued to work with the mother and the school psychologist to design a traditional behavioral plan. It identified five basic behaviors (i.e., talk in a softer voice, stay on task, keep hands to self, etc.) for Andrew to focus on controlling. On a chart, we divided the day into seven time periods. Andrew was to receive a *yes* or *no* for each behavior during each time slot. For a day to be considered "successful," he had to accumulate 30 yes notations out of a possible 35, and a successful day granted privileges at home each evening.

The plan hadn't been in place for very long (it was semi-successful, and behaviors were improving somewhat) when the mother came into the classroom to announce that we were changing the plan. She had bought Andrew the stereo set of his dreams and put the box in the closet in his bedroom where he could see it every day. When he had gone 30 consecutive days with at least 32 *yeses* per day, he'd get the stereo. The psychologist and I agreed to try it but were both concerned about the message this would give Andrew about getting something for doing what he needed to do. We also wondered about the precedent; what might she buy him next? It took a quite a while for him to manage himself for 30 consecutive days, but eventually he "won" the stereo set.

What happened next was most interesting. By this time, it had become a matter of pride for him to get as many *yeses* per day as possible. During the time he was aiming for the stereo set reward, he had experienced enough success in controlling his behavior that he had come to enjoy that sense of accomplishment. He also saw that when he had his actions under control, other students responded more positively toward him, and friendships began to develop. He had started out with strictly extrinsic motivation: he wanted that stereo set! But somewhere in the middle, that intrinsic motivation began to develop. He was compelled to do the right things because doing them, he said, "felt good inside me." And isn't that what we hope for all our students to experience and continue to experience through their lives?

Creating Ways to Celebrate

Schools grapple with decisions about how to inspire students to *become* respectful, responsible, and self-regulated in their academic and personal behavior and to celebrate when their actions show these qualities. We've noted that there are unlimited ways teachers, students, and all adults in the school can celebrate progress and success in *belonging* and *becoming* every day.

A School-Wide Plan for Celebrating Student Successes

In addition to these practices—which become a normal part of the daily routine—many schools establish school-wide systems for motivating and celebrating student successes (academic, behavioral, or both). Task forces or committees put their heads together to create (or adapt) all sorts of plans to fit their unique school communities. There is no one "best" way to do this. Your school needs a plan that meets the needs of your students and works to further your own goals.

If we want our students to feel that their school and classrooms are places where they can *belong* and have a say, and if we truly value their voices and leadership abilities, then it is critical to bring them into the process of designing such a program. This seems especially fitting when the decisions have to do with practices that affect virtually every aspect of their school lives. So design or re-examine your school-wide practices hand-in-hand with your middle level students.

In a summary report on student motivation, the Center on Education Policy (2012) urged educators to "think carefully about the pros and cons of instituting a reward program to spur students' motivation" (p. 8). They shared some characteristics to consider if the school does institute such a program. Among them are:

- Reward students for mastering specific skills or increasing understanding rather than for reaching a level of performance.

- Reward behaviors or tasks that are clear and that students believe are within their control and achievable.

- Reward tasks that are challenging enough to hold interest but not so challenging that they lead students to feel incompetent.

- If possible, offer rewards linked to academics (such as books).

- Allow students to opt out of pursuing a reward.

- Give rewards promptly so that they are clearly connected to the student's action.

- Choose individuals to give out the rewards who are socially important to students.

- Avoid conditioning students to depend on a reward.

- Target behaviors or tasks that students feel are achievable, clearly articulated, and within their control.

- See that teachers receive professional development on student motivation (pp. 8-9).

We would add:

- Develop tools and processes to monitor and evaluate the program. Include students in the evaluation and decisions that are made from the results of the evaluations.

At my (Laurie) previous school, we used what we called the CATS Cash program. (We saw a similar program and adapted it to fit our needs.) CATS was an acronym for the components of our standards for student success (see Figure 9-1). We printed paper CATS "cash" and made sure that all adults in the school had some on hand at all times. When a student was "caught" doing something that was part of standards, the adult who witnessed the act would hand her or him a CATS Cash bill. The cash could be exchanged for several rewards, including a positive contact home with parents or guardians (an unexpectedly popular choice for middle school students). See Figure 9-1 below for the list of rewards.

Figure 9-1

Encouraging Positive Behavior

Purpose
The Encouraging Positive Behavior program is designed to foster a climate of safety, success, cooperation, academic excellence, responsibility, and respect for everyone who enters our doors. We believe that all CATS should uphold the Standards for Student Success at all times.

Standards for Student Success
Continue to Succeed
Achieve Learning Goals
Take Responsibility
Show Respect

Student Incentives (CATS Cash)
1 CATS CASH
Name Entered in Monthly Drawing (for items listed below)
Positive Phone Call Home from Staff Member of Your Choice

5 CATS CASH
Free School Pen
Free Slushy, Cookie, or Iced Tea at Lunch
Free Candy or Drink at School Event

10 CATS CASH
Eat Lunch with a Friend in Lunchroom (same grade level)
Free Item from the School Store

15 CATS CASH
Free School Athletic Event or Dance Pass

20 CATS CASH
Free School Spirit Item

30 CATS CASH
(for all students who earn at least 30 CATS CASH for semester)

CATS Cash Celebration

To help our younger students make a successful transition to middle school, we added a feature to the program for the sixth graders designed to help them track their own success. This weekly chart (printed on a card) called "Making CATS Tracks" (Figure 9-2) encouraged students to *become* responsible students and learners. Students carried their "Making CATS Tracks" cards to their common academic classes each day. Expectations were listed on the card, and every student who met the expectations received a stamp in the day's box from that team teacher. One stamp per class in four classes per day for 10 days equaled the opportunity to earn 40 stamps for each card. If students earned 36 out of the 40 possible stamps, they earned the opportunity to go to small celebrations on Fridays (typically lasting 15-30 minutes). These celebrations resembled a structured recess time, giving them a short opportunity to have fun with friends (and to be active and move!). It was especially effective with younger students who were adjusting to new transitions and routines.

Figure 9-2

Making CATS Tracks

Name:				You can miss 4 stamps. You must have 36 stamps to participate in Fun Friday.				Dates:		
Homeroom:										

	Mon	Tues	Wed	Thur	Fri	Mon	Tues	Wed	Thur	Fri	Goals & Expectations
3rd Period											1. Prepared for Class
4th Period											2. Completed Assignments
5th Period											3. On Track Behavior
6th Period											

Outstanding CATS			
C	Continue to Succeed	Parent Signature —Week 1	Week 1 Comments
A	Achieve Learning Goals		
T	Take Responsibility	Parent Signature —Week 2	Week 2 Comments
S	Show Respect		

Celebration for Self-Regulation

Consider recognizing students who have no discipline referrals and who are proficient in or passing all classes for a grading period (every mid-quarter, every quarter, or every semester). Reserve some time for these students to be celebrated with an opportunity to socialize with peers in a structured and supervised environment or some other simple recognition. A key to this type of recognition is that discipline and proficiencies or grades start over each assessment period and are not held against a student for a future assessment period. What we want to do is teach students to monitor themselves and to work toward improvement, and that includes giving students second chances (do-overs and retakes) when appropriate.

More Celebrations

There are also less formal ways to recognize student behavioral and academic accomplishments. No one plan will work for every school; adapt ideas to fit the culture and needs of your school. Here are a few ideas that we have used or collected over the years:

> **Positive Mail**—Design and print off a variety of simple postcards so staff can easily mail a positive note to parents. To expand on this idea, print a set of mailing labels, and leave them in the staff room along with enough postcards for all students. Challenge the staff to write and send a positive note to the parents of every child during the next two-week period.

> **Purple Tickets** (you choose the color)—Each week, each staff member finds a ticket and a postcard in his or her mailbox. These are used to recognize students (more postcards and tickets are available upon request). The teacher writes a positive note about the student (with specifics about accomplishments). The student is given the ticket to bring to the office for a drawing. On Thursday, two names are chosen from the jar. Those students invite any staff member of their choice to lunch the next day. Arrange for local restaurants to donate lunches!

Shout Out the News—Publicize news about school and non-school achievements in your bulletin, school newspaper, website, school social media page, and parent newsletter. Make sure this bragging includes a wide variety of accomplishments in many areas of *belonging* and *becoming*.

Lunch with the Principal, Donuts with the Deans, Cookies with the Counselor (you get the idea)—Ask teachers to watch for instances where students use their voices to make positive contributions to the school community or to speak up for other students. Select three to five of these students each week to meet with a school "official" and discuss their reflections and suggestions about what's working well at the school and what needs improvement.

Lunchtime Recognition—Playground and cafeteria supervisors have tickets to give to students who are seen cleaning up after themselves or others or doing another helpful or respectful deed. Tickets are put into a drawing for a small prize at the end of the week.

Be Creative—Don't limit formal recognition to academics or highly visible accomplishments. Give awards for being a good friend, showing responsibility, bouncing back from difficulty, making improvement, helping someone *belong*, helping to make the school a safe place, etc.

When a school builds a culture of positive recognition—recognition for multiple indications of *belonging* and *becoming*—every student (many of whom might not be recognized otherwise) can have many chances to feel validated and affirmed within his or her school. When we add the school-wide program to all the possibilities described at the beginning of this chapter for celebration in classrooms and other

> **If there are enough qualities and categories that you're noticing, there will be chances for all students to be "caught" meeting the criteria for success.**

activities, all students can feel themselves living in a community of validation. For an all-school program to be successful, the standards for specific recognitions should be well considered and clearly stated. So, here are a few words of caution: Do not lower standards in an effort to include more students; the recognition must be authentic. False praise is worse than no praise at all. Students will rise to meet the expectations you set when they know that you believe they can do it. If there are enough qualities and categories that you're noticing, there will be chances for all students to be "caught" meeting the criteria for success.

Out-of-School Accomplishments

While it is admittedly easier to celebrate students' accomplishments that happen at school, you will build bridges of goodwill with families and the community when you recognize accomplishments that occur outside school as well. Many students participate in non-school clubs and events such as 4H, scouts, arts, dance and other athletics, volunteer activities, and community service events. Some of the most astounding advances in *belonging* and *becoming* occur in experiences outside the school walls.

Find a way to encourage students and families to share good news from the outside world. This can include such ideas as having a hallway bulletin board designated to post news articles and pictures about students' accomplishments, using a display cabinet for short-term displays of trophies, ribbons, and other displays or inserting out-of-school accomplishments into the reading of the daily bulletin or morning announcements. Not only do such methods recognize students for their efforts beyond school, but they also help staff members and students learn more about individual students and deepen student-teacher and school-family relationships. The "accomplishments" celebrated in this way don't have to be all about winning competitions or getting awards. Show off anything students are doing that demonstrates efforts to *belong* or *become*.

Communicating Successes

Sadly, today's young adolescents frequently get a bad rap. Too often they are portrayed in the media as rude, self-centered, and uncaring. Descriptors such as *immature, moody, or hormones on wheels* are often used to describe this age group. And, while these generalizations do contain some elements of truth, if taken as gospel, they discount the complexity of the age group. Young adolescents are experiencing rapid physical and emotional change as they struggle along the road to independence, and for those reasons they can be contradictory at times—confused or confident, awkward or articulate, passive or passionate. But those of us who work with young adolescents know just how concerned, caring, and compassionate they can be.

So why, then, does the general public have such a poor impression of middle schoolers? Perhaps it's because we remember incidents that reinforce our beliefs. For example, when we see young adolescents being rude, it validates our perceptions, and we're more likely to remember it than when we see them being polite. Unfortunately, young adolescents, themselves, recognize this typecasting and are disturbed by their public images.

We must actively communicate our students' and school's successes. Enlist a staff member in your grade level, on your team, or in your department to take responsibility for sharing the school's and students' good news; this is essential to forming an accurate perception of your school and students within the wider community. Another staff member or a group of students can take on the task of posting newspaper or online articles in the hallways about any positive school or student event. Assign someone to write one article per week or month for your local newspaper, highlighting some exciting growth or events at the school. Send a yearly invitation to legislators who represent your school asking them to visit classrooms and see the great work teachers and students are doing. Call the local television station and invite them to see your "A" Day (see Chapter 5). Invite local realtors in for breakfast and have students share why your school is a great place to attend. Give a presentation of the school's accomplishments in the areas of attendance, attitude (citizenship), academics, arts, and athletics—or in any other areas of *belonging* or *becoming* you identify—to the school board. If you don't tell your story, someone else will (and you might not like what she says!).

Putting It into Practice

As an individual, team, small group, or entire staff, use some of these activities to spark discussions, reflect on your current practices or situations, listen to others, or set goals.

1. As a staff, make a list of the different ways you celebrate your students (and staff!). How does your school ensure that all students are recognized in the different areas that help make a student successful? How can your school improve in this area?

2. Consider the following statement: By celebrating what's right, we find the energy to fix what's wrong. Do you think that focusing on the positive can give the energy to fix what's not right, or should we concentrate on what's wrong if we want to fix it? Why or why not? How does this idea play out at our school? In our classrooms? Is there a difference? Should there be?

3. Collect as much data as you can on which students are being honored and celebrated at your school. Is it primarily athletes and honor-roll students? Is it balanced across gender, grade level, ethnicity, academic performance, etc.? Are students recognized for growth or primarily for achievement? Use the data to determine areas for improvement.

4. Review this chapter's section on Recognizing and Rewarding Thoughtfully. With a team or grade-level group, discuss the research findings about intrinsic and extrinsic motivation, praise, and rewards. Identify practices and language-changes that you can make to avoid dampening students' intrinsic motivation. Hold the same discussion with students. Listen to their reflections about the value and effects of different kinds of rewards and recognitions. Ask students to contribute new ideas about how to celebrate *belonging* and *becoming*.

Conclusion

In Their Own Voices

"When you *belong*, you never have to sit alone at lunch."

"When I experience myself *becoming* in some way, I feel that I am on top of the world."

- The words of two middle grades students

Listen to students describe what it means to *belong* and *become* and why these matter to them and their peers.

To belong (in my school and in my classes) means
You are accepted as a person.
You have friends that you feel safe around.
You're not alone when you leave class.
You perform better because you know people and people know you.
You fit in.
You have someone to walk to class with.
You are never alone at lunch or recess.
You are energized.
You have friends who support you, and you support them.
People talk to you.
You are happy with your work, friends, and education.
You are welcomed and involved.

Here's why it matters to have a sense of **belonging** at school:

It affects everything! It affects your motivation to do anything!

You are confident.

You will do better in school, which will help you to belong more.

If you don't feel you belong, your confidence and social skills suffer.

It's easier to focus on learning. Otherwise you will spend all your time and energy stressing about not belonging.

Without it, you have no energy for learning.

When you don't belong, nothing else seems to matter at all.

Without a sense of belonging, you are empty.

When you don't belong, you don't care, you don't try, you don't want to finish your work.

It is absolutely necessary for your overall happiness, self-esteem, and mental health.

To become (in ways that students can do in school), means

Achieving the best you can, even exceeding what is expected of you.

Believing in your own actions.

Believing that you can learn, think, and act responsibly on your own.

Taking risks to go for more than is necessary.

Building from your mistakes.

Finding friends that will include you.

Achieving your own goals.

Working hard and being nice.

Getting prepared for high school.

Persevering.

Developing socially—reaching out to others and getting along with others.

Being who you are.

With the help of the school and the people in it, middle grades kids can **become**

Harder workers who persevere and try.

People who will make good choices.

Better able to express themselves and speak up for themselves.

More aware of and more caring of other people's feelings.

Intelligent and experienced.

People who are not content with just passing grades.

The best that they can be.

Whatever they want to be.

Better people.

This is our hope for our readers—our fellow-adventurers in loving and educating young adolescents: that for every program you design, every lesson you plan, every new procedure you consider, or every goal—for everything that you do now or think about doing—you will (individually and with your colleagues) ask,

Will this help our students *belong* or *become*, or both?

One of the best ways to find out how your plans, programs, processes, and procedures affect your students is to ask them. Remember, always, that their voices tell you things you can learn from no other sources. They know things we educators don't know. And often, we won't find these things out from them until we ask.

Shortly after the two of us had the epiphany about the all-encompassing concepts of *belonging* and *becoming* and began to explore how to put that into words and action, we realized we needed to hear from students. We gathered groups of sixth through eighth graders; the groups were as heterogeneously mixed as we could possibly create. With all groups combined into one large group, we held a short (15 minutes) general discussion to start students thinking about *belonging* and *becoming*. We asked them to think about what the terms and concepts meant in the context of their school. We encouraged them to think about their own experiences with each of the concepts. Then we sent them off by themselves with an anonymous written survey and gave them about 30 minutes to reflect on the topics and express their ideas.

This was just the right beginning for us, and we believe it would be for any school's or teacher's journey with the partnership of *belonging* and *becoming*! What we learned from students has helped to shape our own interests and directions in this book and in our work with students. The experience brought us new insights into students' perceptions of the school community, students' beliefs about themselves and each other, the power of their voices, their positive mindsets and optimism, their hope, and their wisdom. It gave us a fresh look at our choices and practices. The experience brought students an opportunity to dig into themselves, express their opinions, share their lives (some of it behind-the-scenes), and have a say.

We highly recommend that you explore these topics with your students, for your benefit and theirs. This can be done on a classroom level, a team (or grade) level, or as all-school research. (And it is research—as valuable as any other school-improvement research you could do!) We've included some sample reflection surveys, "My Thoughts About *Belonging*" and "My Thoughts About *Becoming*," (Appendix F-1 and Appendix F-2) on pages 242. But you can design surveys that fit your students or solicit this information in other ways. Ask about the things you need to learn from your students.

We chose a process that combined discussion with individual reflection so students could warm up to the concepts with adult involvement but be able to reflect without influence from other students (or give answers they thought might please the adult). We recommend that sessions tackle these two concepts separately. You might involve more students by forming different groups for each of the two topics. We also recommend that you take action on what you learn from the survey and then repeat the survey again during the year(s) to re-assess students' experiences of *belonging* and *becoming* in their school.

In addition to asking students to share what *belonging* and *becoming* mean, our survey asked students to reflect on some items related to the manifestations and experiences of *belonging* (or not *belonging*) and *becoming* (or not *becoming*). These are some of the students' reflections:

Here's how someone can tell that he or she **belongs**:

They have someone to sit with at lunch.

They are not alone at recess.

They are not alone in the hall.

They have people to talk to when they get to class.

They are confident around their classmates.

They laugh.

When you do NOT have a sense of **belonging**,

It is absolutely the most horrible feeling.

You feel discarded.

You think the whole world is against you.

You feel insecure, sad, edgy, and hopeless.

Your gut goes empty and your brain is just thinking of the worst things in life.

You feel paranoid, not knowing what other people are saying about you.

You feel that you have no place in school or life.

It feels as if you've been abandoned in a forest, having to fend for yourself.

You feel lonely, like nobody wants you.

You think you are worthless—not a good person.

It just feels like crap. There's no other way to describe it!

Here's how I can tell if someone does NOT have a **sense of belonging**:

They look constantly disappointed.

They sit alone at lunch.

They are alone at recess.

They avoid other kids.

They don't talk to anyone.

They don't care about their grades.

They are the ones that get bullied.

They look depressed.

They walk with their heads down. They are always staring down.

I can tell if I am *becoming* (in any of the ways I think I could **become** at school) by

How much I feel at home.

My success in my classes.

How outgoing I feel.

Improvement in my grades.

Increased confidence in my ability to think, learn, and do my work.

Improvement in my attitudes.

Good experiences at my parent-teacher-student conferences.

Noticing that people react to me positively.

Whether I'm achieving my goals.
Whether I'm doing even more that I expected.
How much I am welcoming kids that are being left out or put down.

When I experience myself **becoming** in some way, I feel:
A little brighter.
Accomplished, proud, and maybe even excited.
Motivated—like I can do anything.
That I am on top of the world.
Proud that I am appreciated and my work is noticed.
That I am a better and more well-thought-of person.
Happy and full.
Higher self-esteem and self-confidence.

When a student does NOT experience success at **becoming**,
They might feel like giving up on life.
They have zero confidence.
They have no self-belief.
They cry.
They withdraw.
They can feel angry, depressed, or suicidal.

Belonging and *becoming* are not passive verbs! They are not things teachers and schools do to or for their students. Of course, we can create communities, design activities and situations, train our teachers, lend support, and teach skills that help with both processes—that's what middle school is all about. But the student herself or himself must be actively involved in his or her own *belonging* and *becoming*. As much as we'd like to, we can't magically make a student feel included, have satisfying relationships with peers, be self-motivated, or feel competent in schoolwork. Students are not pawns in these processes. *Belonging* is not the same as having adult acceptance. *Becoming* is not just doing everything the teacher asks or learning everything to the extent that the adults approve. We need to help our students understand that *belonging* and *becoming* are:

- Gradual (they take time).
- Current (they're happening now; they're not things that will happen only in the future).
- Participatory (the student must take an active role).

Part of the role of teachers is to help students find ways to be active in their own *belonging* and *becoming*. We urge you to watch for opportunities to do that. In addition, appreciate the large role that students have in helping each other with these processes. With many of the qualities, attitudes, and behaviors involved in *belonging* and *becoming*, students can actually be far more helpful and influential than adults. Confirm and re-confirm the message to students that everyone in the school should be involved in helping **everyone** *belong* and *become*.

Our survey asked students to reflect on and recall what they have done (and can do) to help other kids *belong* or *become* and to help themselves increase in *belonging* and *becoming*. We learned that many of the students were consciously taking an active role in *belonging* and *becoming* for themselves and others. We found they had no shortage of ideas and actual deeds to recount. This helped us learn what behaviors we could teach, encourage, and strengthen. Here are some of the things students had to say:

The best things kids can do to help other kids **belong** are
> *Just be kind.*
> *Invite them into their group at lunch.*
> *Hang out with them at recess.*
> *Don't let anyone have to be alone in the hall.*
> *If you see someone sitting alone, move over and talk to them.*
> *Try to help them not feel awkward.*
> *Choose to work in a group with them.*
> *Just go for it. Talk to people.*
> *Sit at a table by them without being invited.*
> *Stand up to things that are not right that you see happening to someone.*
> *Do not judge them.*
> *Stop just thinking about themselves and think about others.*

Something I've done to help someone else **belong** is
Starting up a conversation.
Volunteering to be their partner in an activity.
Asking someone to sit with me when I saw him looking sad.
Inviting them to sit with my group at lunch.
Answering their questions.
Showing them to class.
Putting myself in their shoes.
Including them in a project I was doing.
Moving to someone's table at lunch (empty except for him).
Getting my friends to include someone at recess.

Something I've done to increase my own sense **of belonging** is
Asked people to sit with me at lunch.
Started saying hi and giving a smile to a lot more people.
Joined a soccer team.
Started being kinder to people.
Took up an attitude of treating others the way I wanted to be treated.
Tried to be more sociable, even though it was scary.
Started getting my homework done sooner so I'd have time for making new friends.
Just bit the bullet and sat at a lunch table with people I didn't know.
Talked to people I don't know well.
Tried to be more open-minded about who I could be friends with.
Joined an after-school club.
Worked at being positive and thankful for the things I already have.
Asked to be in a group school project, knowing it would help myself.

The best things students can do to help other students to **become** are
Listen in class and try hard—to be an example to other students.
Help them belong, because that motivates them to become.
Support their efforts by giving them attention and compliments.
Don't make fun of them or insult them.
Don't laugh at their questions or answers.
Include them in groups and activities.
Ask them questions to help them show what they know.
Help them if they're having trouble with something.
Ask them to help you with something.
Be kind.

The best thing I have done to help another student **become** is
Sitting with them at lunch.
Being friendly and supportive.
Introducing myself and helping them with the class.
Pushing them a little past their comfort zone.
Complimenting them.
Helping to motivate them to do their best.
Helping them ask for help.
Asking them to explain something to me.
Help them on things they are having trouble with.
Talking to them when they're feeling put down.
Sticking up for them when they're being bullied.

The best things I can do to help myself to **become** are to:
Work to keep good relationships with my friends.
Make a list of things to do because visualizing helps me achieve my goals.
Never give up.
Never hold grudges.
Not be afraid to ask questions in class.
Believe in myself.
Look at myself in the third person and observe what I need to work on
    (like focusing in class or saying nice things to people).
Persevere.
Go for my full potential.
Pay attention in class.
Never exclude people.
Make others feel good about themselves.
Look ahead and see how something will help me in the future.

The survey also gave students opportunities to reflect on things they observed in their school that were helping students *belong* and *become*, as well as things the school could do better. Students told us:

The best thing I've seen a teacher do to help a student **belong** is
Let kids do learning activities that they think of themselves.
Make students laugh and laugh with them.
Help everyone in the class practice social skills.
Mix up groups so students have a chance to make friends.
Guide students into groups where they'll work best.
Never let students choose their own seats.

Always see that everyone is involved in every activity.
Let students know that she accepts them all equally.
Give someone a friend to tour the school with all day.
Ask individual students how they are doing.
Talk to every student every day.
Just notice when students need help, even when they don't ask.
Help students believe in themselves.
Show trust in the students.

These things work AGAINST everyone feeling a **sense of belonging** at school:
Exclusiveness of groups.
A lot of attention to the popular people.
Cliques.
Name-calling.
Students whispering behind other students' backs.
Bullying.
Students getting away with making fun of other students.
The school not being open to suggestions or changes.

To help ALL kids at my school feel that they **belong**, I would change this:
I would take away the invisible line that divides people into groups and cliques.
Teachers should stop letting kids choose groups.
We need bigger tables at lunch. The round tables hold few people and it's easy for kids to be excluded.
I would make a school where everybody feels included.
The adults in the school would recognize the students and talk to them.
The school could be more inviting.
There should be a welcoming committee that meets with new students for pizza or lunch and helps them make friends.
I would find a way to put a stop to these: mean nicknames, making fun, using negative words, and excluding others.
I'd like to see that everyone has a group that they like and are comfortable.
Add a class for all students to practice social skills and learn about other people.

Things that have happened in school that have MOST helped me to **become** are:
Good friends and good teachers.
Learning to be supportive of other people.
Setting high standards for myself.

Helpful teachers and worthwhile assignments.

Learning to ask for help.

Teachers pushing me to try harder things.

Being encouraged to learn new things outside of school.

People helping me when I am confused.

People treating me with respect.

People being nice and kind.

People encouraging me to be nice and kind.

People including me and inviting me to join them.

Putting me in a group of people that I don't usually hang out with so I could learn from them.

Getting help with my problems and questions, no matter how dumb they are.

The best things a teacher can do to help students to **become** are

Listening—really listening.

Encouraging them to learn beyond school.

Challenging them to reach beyond what they thought they could do.

Congratulating them on their achievements.

Listening to what they have to say.

Including them in decisions.

Explaining things they don't understand, even if it takes a few tries.

Telling them to believe they can improve.

Assigning alternatives to be at their learning levels and paces.

Exploring their talents.

Not embarrassing them in front of others if they do something wrong.

Not making them feel bad or stupid when they ask a question or don't know an answer.

To help ALL kids at my school feel that they are **becoming,** I would change this:

I'd put more pressure on them to succeed.

All students should have help with social skills.

Every student would receive a compliment a day.

I would never let kids choose their own groups for group work in class.

The school should offer a class where students could talk about their short-term and long-term goals.

Make sure that the school has advisors for all kids to talk to.

Add more group activities that help to make and improve friendships.

See that all students have a chance to be heard.

Include a daily goal with the morning announcements.

Have the kinds of learning activities that involve everyone.

I would ban cliques, exclusion, pulling pranks, and laughing at others.

Give more encouragement for people to think outside themselves.
Make absolutely sure that teachers are there for students and support them.
There shouldn't be any students in the school who feel nobody believes
in them.

We're awed by the students' honesty, their sensitivity to human needs, their insights into themselves and others. It was interesting to see how many of their responses mixed aspects of *belonging* and *becoming*; it showed us how entwined the two are in their experience. We're delighted to see the school through their eyes (even if they reveal some flaws or weaknesses). There's not anything they told us that we didn't need to hear, that didn't teach us something new, or that didn't reaffirm something we did know. These students, without knowing it, gave us a list of topics and practices to consider, add, or re-examine and several issues to discuss. Their insights taught us what to celebrate and what to work on.

For example, we could not ignore the number of times we read about having someone (or no one) to sit with at lunch or be with at recess or the idea that students need someone to talk to them. We saw the words *kind, inclusion, compliment, believe in myself, support, challenge* repeated throughout their reflections. We read, more than once, that students don't want to be in a culture where others are made fun of, talked about, or bullied. We noticed they feel that letting students choose their own groups for academic group work interferes with *belonging* and *becoming*. We saw that students asked for more teaching of social skills. We can go right to work on finding practices to address these needs. Wouldn't it be wonderful if we could have a school where nobody sits alone at lunch! Think of how far that would go toward helping the young adolescents in the school feel a sense of *belonging* that removes impediments to their *becoming*! We guess that this is an issue in every middle level school. What a goal to set! And if we get anywhere close to meeting it—what an accomplishment to celebrate!

We hope that you embrace the concepts of *belonging* and *becoming* as the heart of the mission and the work you do with young adolescents and make this powerful duo a motto for your school or your classroom (or both)! We hope that this will give you new glasses through which to see your practices and programs. And we hope you'll begin by asking the students—a practice that gives them a meaningful way to matter and make a difference. Listen to your students' reflections, take them seriously, and work to act on what you learn. When you do, you'll accelerate your success at making your school and classrooms places where students can truly *belong* and *become*—not just when they get into high school, college, and adulthood—but starting right now!

Appendix A
Characteristics of Young Adolescents

This special section on the characteristics of young adolescents originally appeared in This We Believe: Keys to Educating Young Adolescents *and was prepared by Dr. Peter C. Scales, senior fellow, Office of the President, Search Institute. Dr. Scales, a developmental psychologist, author, speaker, and researcher, is widely recognized as one of the nation's foremost authorities on adolescent development. His recent studies have focused on identifying and promoting "developmental assets," those conditions that are linked to young people's success in school and in life. Middle grades educators are in a unique position to help build these developmental assets such as feeling empowered, playing useful roles, building social competence, and developing a commitment to learning, all of which are goals of middle level education.*

In the area of physical development, young adolescents

- Experience rapid, irregular physical growth.
- Undergo bodily changes that may cause awkward, uncoordinated movements.
- Have varying maturity rates, with girls tending to begin puberty one and one-half to two years earlier than boys, and young adolescents in some cultural groups tending to begin puberty earlier than those in other groups. (African American youth, for example, begin puberty earlier than European-American youth, on average.)
- Experience restlessness and fatigue due to hormonal changes.
- Need daily physical activity because of increased energy, and if not engaged in regular physical activity, often lack fitness, with poor levels of endurance, strength, and flexibility.
- Need to release energy, often in sudden, apparently meaningless, outbursts of activity.
- Have preferences for junk food but need good nutrition.
- May be prone to risky dieting practices in order to lose or gain weight (a practice found specifically prevalent among European-American youth).
- Continue to develop sexual awareness, which increases with the onset of menstruation, the growth spurt, and appearance of secondary sex characteristics.

- Are concerned with bodily changes that accompany sexual maturation and changes resulting in an increase in nose size, protruding ears, long arms, and awkward posture, concerns magnified because of comparison with peers.

- Have an increased need for comprehensive, medically accurate education about sexuality and health issues that responds to these increased concerns.

- Are physically vulnerable because they may adopt poor health habits or engage in experimentation with alcohol and other drugs and high-risk sexual behaviors.

In the area of cognitive-intellectual development, young adolescents

- Display a wide range of individual intellectual development.

- Increasingly are able to think abstractly, not only concretely; both concrete and abstract thinking styles may be evident in the same young adolescent, depending on the issue or situation.

- Commonly face decisions that require more sophisticated cognitive and social-emotional skills.

- Are intensely curious and have a wide range of intellectual pursuits, although few are, or need to be, sustained.

- Prefer active over passive learning experiences; depending on their cultural backgrounds, some young adolescents might be quite engaged in learning through observation but might not always show this engagement through the active participation that is typically desired and rewarded by teachers (these learning and participation strategies have been noted as more common among Native American students, for example).

- Prefer interaction with peers during learning activities.

- May show disinterest in conventional academic subjects but are intellectually curious about the world and themselves.

- Respond positively to opportunities to connect what they are learning to participation in real-life situations such as community service projects. Research has shown that such experiences may be particularly valuable in helping students from lower-income backgrounds become more engaged with school.

- Develop an increasingly more accurate understanding of their current personal abilities but may prematurely close doors to further exploration in particular interest areas due to feeling inadequate in comparison to peers.

- Are developing a capacity to understand higher levels of humor, some of which may be misunderstood by adults to be overly sarcastic or even aggressive.
- Are inquisitive about adults and are keen observers of them; depending on their cultural upbringing, some young adults also may often challenge adults' authority.

In the area of moral development, young adolescents

- Are in transition from moral reasoning that focuses on "what's in it for me" to consideration of the feelings and rights of others; self-centered moral reasoning may be in evidence at the same time as principle-oriented reasoning, depending on the circumstances; cultural differences in the socialization of moral development, especially among young adolescents whose families are recent immigrants, may contribute to special moral conflicts or developments for those young people attempting to navigate multiple cultures.
- Increasingly are capable of assessing moral matters in shades of grey as opposed to viewing them in black and white terms more characteristic of young children; however, this increased potential for more complex moral reasoning may often not be evident in practice.
- Are generally idealistic, desiring to make the world a better place and to make a meaningful contribution to a cause or issue larger than themselves.
- Often show compassion for those who are downtrodden or suffering and have a special concern for animals and the environmental problems that our world faces.
- Are capable of and value direct experience in participatory democracy.
- Owing to their lack of experience, are often impatient with the pace of change, underestimating the difficulties in making desired social changes.
- Are likely to believe in and espouse values such as honesty, responsibility, and cultural acceptance, while at the same time learning that they and the people they admire can also be morally inconsistent, and can lie or cheat, avoid responsibility, and be intolerant.
- At times, are quick to see flaws in others but slow to acknowledge their own faults
- Are often interested in exploring spiritual matters as a part of growing their awareness of self and the world, the connection between self and others, and the development of a life of hope and purpose, even as they may become distant from formal religious organizations; for many, however,

connections to religious organizations may continue to be a vital part of early adolescence, such as among African American youth for whom religious connections have been found to be a particular source of strength.

- Are moving from acceptance of adult moral judgments to developing their own values; nevertheless, they tend to embrace major values consistent with those of their parents and other valued adults.

- Rely on parents and significant adults for advice, especially when facing major decisions.

- Greatly need and are influenced by adult role models who will listen to them and affirm their moral consciousness and actions.

- Are increasingly aware of, concerned with, and vocal about inconsistencies between values exhibited by adults and conditions they see in society.

In the area of psychological development, young adolescents are

- Often preoccupied with self, an intersection between psychological and spiritual development as they awaken to or become aware of their true essence or spirit.

- Seek to become increasingly independent, searching for adult identity and acceptance, but continue to need support and boundary-setting from adults; the search for independence may be stronger among youth who have been socialized in European-American cultures, whereas young adolescents from some cultural backgrounds such as Hispanic or Asian-American youth, may be as or more focused on social obligations and roles in the family and other groups than they are on independence.

- May experience a significant increase in the awareness of and the importance they give to their ethnic identity.

- Experience levels of self-esteem that may fluctuate up and down but in general are adequate and increase over time; in contrast, levels of self-confidence in academic subjects, sports, and creative activities often decline significantly from the levels of middle childhood.

- Typically get passionately and deeply involved with at least one talent, interest, or hobby that becomes a "spark" in their lives, giving them energy, joy, purpose, direction, and focus (but may need help identifying such sparks or passionate interests). Students from more economically disadvantaged backgrounds may be less able than more affluent students to identify their sparks unless schools maintain free or low-cost co-curricular programs that provide equity of access to these opportunities.

- Believe that personal problems, feelings, and experiences are unique to themselves.
- Tend to be self-conscious and highly sensitive to personal criticism.
- Desire recognition for their positive efforts and achievements.
- Increasingly behave in ways associated with their sex as traditional sex role identification strengthens for most young adolescents; some young adolescents may question their sexual identities.
- Are curious about sex and have sexual feelings; they need to know that these are normal.
- Are psychologically vulnerable, because at no other stage in development are they more likely to encounter and be aware of so any differences between themselves and others.
- Are also psychologically resilient; across diversities in race and ethnicity, residence, or socioeconomic status, young adolescents tend to be optimistic and have a generally positive view of their personal future.

In the area of social-emotional development, young adolescents

- Have a strong need for approval and may be easily discouraged.
- Are increasingly concerned about peer acceptance.
- Often overreact to what many adults would consider relatively minor experiences of ridicule, embarrassment, and rejection.
- Although most young adolescents experience some of these discomforts as a typical part of growing up, other students can experience serious and harmful harassment, ridicule, and rejection (which decrease their feelings of safety at and engagement with school) due to their actual or perceived sexual orientation, religious background, immigrant or language status, or level of affluence.
- Are dependent on the beliefs and values of parents and other valued adults but seek to make more of their own decisions.
- Increasingly welcome and benefit from positive relationships with adults outside their families, such as coaches, teachers, spiritual leaders, and neighbors, especially when these adults encourage, support, and nurture young adolescents' pursuit of their sparks and passionate interests.
- Enjoy fads, especially those shunned by adults.
- Have a strong need to belong to a group, with approval of peers becoming as important as adult approval and on some matters even more important.

- Need moderate amounts of time alone to regroup and reflect on daily experiences.

- In their search for group membership, may experience significant embarrassment, ridicule, or rejection from those in other cliques from which they are excluded.

- Can gravitate toward affiliation with disruptive peers or membership in gangs in order to feel part of a group and to protect their physical safety.

- Experiment with new slang and behaviors as they search for a social position within their group, often discarding these "new identities" at a later date.

- Experience mood swings, often with peaks of intensity and unpredictability.

- May exhibit immature behavior because their social skills and ability to regulate emotions frequently lag behind their cognitive and physical maturity. Among some young adolescents, however, particularly those whose cultural backgrounds value such capacities, their social and emotional skills may be more advanced than their cognitive and physical maturity suggest.

- Must adjust to the social acceptance of early maturing girls and boys, especially if they are maturing at a slower rate.

- If physically maturing earlier than peers, must deal with increased pressure around others' expectations of them, especially about engaging in high-risk behaviors.

- Often begin to experience feelings of sexual or romantic attraction to others, with some having significant or romantic relationships and a sizeable minority experiencing sexual behaviors.

- Are often intimidated and frightened by their first middle grades experience because of the large numbers of students and teachers, the size of the building, and what may be for many their first day-to-day experiences with significant proportions of students who are culturally different from them.

- Are socially vulnerable, because, as they develop their beliefs, attitudes, and values, the emphasis media place on such things as money, fame, power, and beauty (and other majority culture perspectives that most often define those issues) may negatively influence their ideals and values or encourage them to compromise their beliefs.

Appendix B
Individual Development Profile
Suggestions for Use

1. Use the form on the next page (or your own variation of it) to plot information that gives an overview of an individual student's development in several categories at a particular time. Identify the student, the names of the teachers who contribute to the profile, and the date the profile was created. Be careful to keep this and other confidential notations about students in a secure, private place.

2. Choose a method to describe the student in each of the categories.

   A You might use a research-based scale or series of steps. For example (all of these are readily available on the Internet):

   - Piaget's Stages of Cognitive Development

   - Erik Erikson's Stages of Psychosocial Development

   - Four Stages of Puberty (the Tanner stages)

   - Kohlberg's Stages of Moral Development along with Gilligan's Stages of the Ethics of Care

   Note: Carol Gilligan, a colleague of Kohlberg, had reservations about Kohlberg's conclusions in that his research used only male subjects. Her own observations and research led her to believe that females tend to follow a somewhat different path in moral development—one inclined more toward care and responsibility to others than toward decision making based on abstract, impartial reasoning and logic.

   B. Or, use the AMLE list of "Characteristics of Young Adolescents" (reprinted in Appendix A of this book) as a guide to each of these categories. Instead of identifying a stage, you might make observational notes about an individual student to generate a profile in each of the categories of development.

3. You might add other categories—such as those specifically related to *belonging* and aspects of *becoming* such as self-determination, autonomy, self-regulation, and competence.

4. As you work on this, you may find you don't know as much as you could about certain categories. This gives an incentive to dig a little deeper in observing or learning about the student. When you're finished, try to take in the whole picture and let it sink in to give you a deeper understanding of that student. If you work on a team, you might share the profiles with other team members. They may have other information to add, and they'll benefit from getting a closer look at the student, too.

Individual Development Profile

Student Name _____ Date _____

Teacher(s) _____

Developmental Category	Comments or Descriptors
Physical	
Cognitive-Intellectual	
Moral	
Psychological	
Social-emotional	

Note: Add other categories such as sense of belonging, executive function, demonstration of competence, self-determination, or autonomy.

Take Away Science Class?
Not So Fast, Please!
Dr. Betty Crocker

Because so many students at the middle school where I taught science were reading well below grade level, it was proposed to take them out of science classes in order to give them an additional hour of reading instruction. As the science department chair, I was concerned, prompting me to ask, "If they are already unsuccessful in a one-hour reading class, how will giving them an additional hour (that would be taught in a similar manner) improve their ability to read?"

Believing that success leads to increased success, I made the case that science was not an expendable class to be given up to gain extra time for reading instruction but was instead an important subject for all students. I proposed that if students were not succeeding the way they were currently being taught, we needed to change the instruction style rather than doing more of the same. To put my money where my mouth was, I offered to take all the students in question if the other science teachers would take all my higher-performing students. And even though it resulted in a slight increase in students in every science class, they agreed.

All students who had scored 24% or lower in reading on the achievement tests we used at the time were invited to an informal meeting to explain what was happening and give them a choice in the decision. They were promised that assignments would be non-traditional and taught in a style that would help them be more successful, both in science and in reading. They were told that effort would be required and cautioned that a zero would not be allowed and would get them transferred out of the class. "You cannot make an F in this class. Seating is limited, so hold on to yours" was the motto of these new classes. Only three turned down the offer, and one of them asked to join after six weeks. One student dropped out, but after a month he apologized and asked to return. Scheduling changes were made to keep disruptions at a minimum, and the new program began.

Instruction was almost exclusively hands-on with limited writing. The structured format used for written work was designed and followed by all the science teachers. Since we knew struggling students needed precise information, we made a poster for each classroom that illustrated the format. Even the higher-achieving students liked this! Since reading skills were almost non-existent, reading from the text was replaced by a teacher-led conversation on the concept being introduced and was based on a KWL (Know, Want-to-know, Learned) chart. I discovered that these students had a lot of science knowledge but were very restricted in their ability to express or share this knowledge.

There are strong relationships and overlaps between science process skills and reading comprehension skills; observation and inferences (science) are akin to fact or opinion (reading); prediction (science) is akin to asking what happens next in the story (reading). Therefore, the science instruction focused on using correlated skills no matter which science concept was being addressed, and the relationship between what they were learning in science and how they could apply the skills to reading was emphasized.

I also gave direct instruction on such expected behaviors for school success as following rules and interacting positively with peers. (In spite of being in middle school, many students had not learned these unwritten rules and did not understand why they mattered.)

As the students became more engaged in their learning, their reading skills began to improve, they began to get higher grades, and behavior problems dramatically decreased. Additionally, as time passed, teachers who had these students in other content areas began to ask what was happening in my class. It seemed that the positive impact flowed into other classes. And it was especially rewarding when some of my students returned after their first semester in high school to show me report cards with passing grades in several subjects!

Appendix D
Student Leadership Council
Dr. Laurie Barron

The Student Leadership Council was a new idea to intentionally solicit input and feedback from students (who really like giving their opinions!). Initially, the composition of the group (choosing which students should be included) was a little controversial. Teachers and administrators felt it was important that students in this group represent some of the strongest leadership on campus, including students who were using their leadership skills in both positive and not-so-positive ways. Leadership is leadership. Those leading negatively needed opportunities to refocus their leadership on something positive, and we believed that giving them a voice would help them direct their leadership tendencies in ways that would benefit everyone. There were some discussions about not giving a "difficult" student attention by placing her on the Council. But in the end, we all knew we needed to do what was best to support our students, help all of them grow, and not just continually punish a student for his or her poor decisions.

We had 30 students on the Council. Teachers chose ten students per grade level representing all different types of students in the school. We wanted balance in gender, academic ability (including students with disabilities and gifted students), extra-curricular involvement, citizenship, and other areas. I (the principal) half-jokingly told teachers that we wanted five students per grade level that you hope your child brings home to marry one day and five students that you prayed your child would never bring home (and that you'd better invest in now just in case your child chooses that student for a spouse one day!). You get the picture.

I recall the consideration of a student who, during the previous year, had more discipline referrals than any other student in the entire school (that's a lot, by the way). His teacher saw his leadership potential and insisted that he be on the Council. She fought to make sure he had a seat at the table. When placed on the Student Leadership Council the following year, not only did he have only one discipline referral, but he also helped to keep others from making poor decisions and receiving discipline referrals. During class change one afternoon, I was standing at a hallway intersection when the bell rang. Students began filling the halls, when, out of nowhere, several students began squirting water out of water bottles. (The had poked holes in the bottle tops in preparation for this escapade.) Before I could say anything, this young man quickly approached me and stopped my attempt to end the madness. (Picture 300 plus seventh graders in small hallways shooting water randomly through the air). He calmly said, "I've got this, Dr. Barron." In less than 20 seconds, he had taken water bottles away from all offenders (with no back talk or recourse whatsoever) and had all students in class before the tardy bell rang. I stood there, amazed. He wished me a good day and returned to class.

Leadership. He had it, and he needed to use it. Redirecting this one student's negative leadership to positively address school needs had a significant impact on our school, teachers, and students. This all happened because someone reached out to this student, built a relationship with this student, believed in this student, and helped him believe that he could have a positive influence on others. (He also prevented a few altercations, a potential food fight, and several instances of sagging pants). His opinion now mattered, and he knew it.

As a group, the students on the Student Leadership Council met each month to share concerns, suggestions, and celebration ideas contributed by their peers ranging from serious topics such as peer pressure and the overall operation of the school to less serious, yet no less important, topics to middle level students such as hall change and what is served for lunch. By alternating meeting times, students were able to meet as a grade level every other month (sometimes it is best to hear one grade's input separately from another.) and then to meet as a full group in alternate months. This schedule removed students from class less frequently since every other month the meeting took place during their lunchtime. We chose not to meet after school because we didn't ever want someone excluded because he couldn't get a ride home or she would miss basketball practice.

This group once took a survey to help the cafeteria manager determine which (federal regulation approved) cookies to make available. These student leaders were small heroes when students' favorite cookies returned to the menu. We also gave this student leadership group opportunities to work with other school leadership groups such as the school's (staff) leadership team so they could see their voice truly matters. And, we invited others to see this group in action. Along with the school staff leadership team, the Student Leadership Council hosted the state superintendent of schools for lunch and visits to classrooms. These students had evidence that their voices mattered. Authentic audiences showed them and the remainder of the student body that their contributions were valued. At the same time, these experiences and responsibilities held them more accountable for their decisions and the actions resulting from those decisions. This group of students collaboratively led and served others to make a positive difference. They took on a true sense of ownership of their school and enjoyed the satisfaction of taking part in what happened in *their* school.

Appendix E

Students Take the Lead

Dr. Laurie Barron,
Adapted from article originally published in *AMLE Magazine*, October, 2015.

Okay, I admit it. I was a little worried about what they would ask for. If I've learned nothing else after 19 years in education, I certainly know that you should be ready to hear it when you ask for students' opinions.

I know the importance of giving students a voice and allowing students to lead and how important it is to make sure students know we take them seriously and that we value their perceptions, input, and opinions. However, I found that giving students a voice was a little easier for me to implement as a classroom teacher and even as a building-level principal. When I moved to the role of superintendent, my interaction with students understandably decreased, and I had trouble finding ways to seek out students' opinions in relevant and meaningful ways.

After seeing a colleague do something similar, our K-8 district began hosting student-led board work sessions two times per year; one session is hosted by our district's 4th graders and the other by our 8th graders. The work session is led by pairs of students sharing with board of trustees members, administrators, teachers, and parents their ideas of how to help improve our schools and our district.

The process of preparing for and presenting to the board of trustees is a serious one; this takes time and commitment from students and their teachers to make the student-led session a reality (and a success). The work begins long before the board work session when students start preparing in their English language arts class. In collaboration, students spend time learning and applying the content standards for reading, writing, listening, speaking, and viewing. They learn standards in a way that matters to them: by picking something that they don't like or that they want to improve about school and then working to convince others that they have a good idea. In doing this work, they learn and implement skills in researching, developing, and supporting a topic; reasoning and acknowledging opposing views; understanding the conventions of written language; using appropriate vocabulary, figurative language, voice, and mood; using technology to produce writing; presenting findings with appropriate displays of evidence; and engaging the audience (they were impressively convincing in many instances), just to name a few.

One of the most difficult parts of the process is the teachers narrowing it down to ten presentations for students to share at the public board work session. And while this process is a lengthy one, eighth-grade teacher Kara Gronley says it's well worth the effort because it "really provides a platform for student learning that gives them a meaningful and authentic audience. It gives them a real world experience that causes change to happen. It allows for student buy-in due to their suggestions being implemented."

When the work session begins, there are typically ten groups with two students each, for a total of 20 students presenting. In our cozy (and not large) boardroom, we set up five tables. Two groups of students sit at each table, and the other guests sitting at the tables are trustees, administrators, teachers, and parents. Before the students begin, I remind the audience (and myself) that the students are leading this meeting and that it is important for us, as their audience, to maintain a sense of wonder, not make assumptions, show our curiosity, and be open to all ideas students present. I also remind us all that we need to be a good audience and to listen like we mean it (which includes putting away cell phones!). Then, over the next two hours, students share their presentations at their table, and the adults rotate several times to different tables to hear as many presentations as possible.

Perhaps one of the most rewarding aspects of the evening is watching the students' ideas come to fruition. In our two years of hosting student-led board work sessions, these students have made quite an impact. Students have successfully rallied for having new soccer nets installed on the playing fields, lines painted on the pavement for basketball games, alterations to the dress code, new elective classes for journalism and drama, and improvements to the bell system. Their ideas (and persuasive delivery of them) also led to our school fielding our first-ever cross country team last spring and a tree being planted in honor of the eighth-grade class, traditions that will remain far after these students' time with us. When last year's 8th graders actually planted the tree, many students helped dig the hole for the tree, and the entire eighth-grade class gathered when the tree was set in place as Lane Whiteman, the student whose idea it was to plant the tree, spoke to his classmates about why he felt planting the tree was important.

What I learned and continue to learn from these students is that their voice matters, not just because they get to share their input (which is so important for young adolescents who often feel undervalued and like everything keeps happening *to* them instead of *for* them), but also because in allowing them to express their opinions in an open forum, we are teaching them the invaluable lesson of how to appropriately share their input. These young people learn very quickly that sharing that "the dress code stinks" isn't likely to get them anywhere but that sharing specific examples of how they can be responsible with more dress code options might just get the powers-that-be to listen to (and maybe even implement) some of their ideas. No one has yet to ask for anything outlandish or silly, immature or mean-natured. Students have taken the invitation to share their ideas very seriously, and they have not wasted the opportunity.

Perhaps one of our eighth-grade teachers Melissa Hardman says it best: "At this age, sometimes students begin to resent adults, and knowing adults are actually listening to their suggestions helps them believe in adults and gives students the power to make a difference in their school."

Another important point to remember is that students' perceptions, just like all other data, are important not only to listen to but also to seek out and review. Just as with other forms of data (think test scores . . .), different data give us a more rich and valid understanding of our culture and our progress. Who better to receive this data from than students themselves, the ones we are here to serve each day. Students need to know that this is their school, their district. As such, they must take responsibility for helping us to continuously improve. And if we give them this responsibility, we must give them some avenue to help make it possible.

Principal Kim Anderson says that these student-led sessions are impacting their school in ways she never imagined, showing students that "they do have a voice, and when they use it, change can happen. It is empowering and connected to life skills. They can carry these skills to the real world. And, this process is directly related to our state curriculum content standards!"

What could have been another typical board work session led by adults or a typical school assignment to write a persuasive essay has been turned into something that is helping to shape not just our schools and our district but the students and adults in them as well. I am honored to be a small part of that.

So, do I still worry sometimes about what ideas our students will come up with next? Not really. I'm far more concerned about what will happen if we ever stop asking them to help us lead and improve.

Appendix F-1
My Thoughts About BELONGING

Think of each of these items as it relates to school.

Answer as many as you can. Don't name any particular student or teacher names.

1. **To belong** (in my school and in my classes) means

2. Here's why it matters for a kid to have a **sense of belonging** at school:

3. Here's how I can tell if someone does NOT have a **sense of belonging**:

4. When someone does NOT have a **sense of belonging**, it feels

5. The best thing I've seen a teacher do to help a student **belong** is

6. The best things kids can do to help other kids **belong** are

7. Something I've done to help someone else **belong** is

8. Something I've done or could do to increase my **own sense of belonging** is

9. To help ALL kids at my school feel that they **belong**, I would change this:

My Thoughts About BECOMING

Think of each of these items as it relates to school.

Answer as many as you can. Don't name any particular student or teacher names.

1. These are some things I think middle school students can **become** with the help of their schools:

2. Here are signs of **becoming** that I already see for myself:

3. When I experience myself **becoming** in some way, I feel

4. When a student does NOT experience success at **becoming**, the effects might be:

5. Things that have happened in school that have MOST helped me to **become** are

6. The best thing I have done to help another student **become** is

7. The best things I can do to help myself to **become** are

8. I've seen these things keep kids from **becoming**:

9. To help ALL kids at my school feel that they are **becoming**, I would change this:

Appendix G
References Cited and Recommended

Allen, K.A., & Bowles, T. (2012). Belonging as a guiding principle in the education of adolescents. *Australian Journal of Educational & Developmental Psychology, 12,* 108-119.

Alexander, W. M. (2011). The junior high school: A changing view. In T. W. Smith & C. K. McEwen (Eds.), *The legacy of middle school leaders: In their own words* (pp. 3-16). Scottsdale, AZ: Information Age Publishing.

Amabile, T. (1996). *Creativity in context.* Boulder, CO: Westview Press.

Anderman, E. M. (2002). School effects on psychological outcomes during adolescence. *Journal of Educational Psychology, 94*(3), 795-809.

Anderman, E. M., & Patrick, H. (2012). Achievement goal theory, conceptualization of ability/intelligence, and classroom climate. In S. Christenson, A. Reschly, & C. Wylie (Eds.), *Handbook of Research on Student Engagement* (pp. 173-191). New York, NY: Springer.

Anderman, L. H. (1999). Classroom goal orientation, school belonging and social goals as predictors of students' positive and negative affect following the transition to middle school. *Journal of Research and Development in Education, 32,* 89–103.

Anderman, L. H. (2003). Academic and social perceptions as predictors of change in middle school students' sense of school belonging. *Journal of Experimental Education, 72,* 5–22.

Arnot, D. (2003). Student voice in school reform: Reframing student-teacher relationships. *McGill Journal of Education, 38*(2), 289-304.

Assor, A., Kaplan, H., & Roth, G. (2002). Choice is good, but relevance is excellent: Autonomy-enhancing and suppressing teacher behaviours predicting students' engagement in schoolwork. *British Journal of Educational Psychology, 72*(2), 261-278.

Bandura, A. (1995). Exercise of personal and collective efficacy changing societies. In A. Bandura (Ed.), *Self-efficacy in changing societies* (pp. 1-45). New York, NY: Cambridge University Press.

Bandura, A. (1997). *Self-efficacy: The exercise of control.* New York, NY: Freeman.

Barron, L. (2015). Students take the lead. *AMLE Magazine, 3*(3), 17-19.

Battistich, V., Solomon, D., Kim, D., Watson, M., & Schaps, E. (1995). Schools as communities, poverty levels of student populations, and students' attitudes, motives, and performance: A multilevel analysis. *American Educational Research Journal, 32,* 627–658.

Battistich, V., Solomon, D., Watson, M., & Schaps, E. (1997). Caring school communities. *Educational Psychologist, 32,* 137-151.

Baumeister, R. F., & Leary, M. R. (1995). The need to belong: Desire for interpersonal attachments as a fundamental human motivation. *Psychological Bulletin, 117,* 497-529.

Beaudoin, N. (2005). *Elevating student voice: How to enhance participation, citizenship, and leadership.* Larchmont, NY: Eye on Education.

Bell, S. (2010). Project-based learning for the 21st century: Skills for the future. *The Clearing House, 83*(2), 39-43.

Berckemeyer, J. (2018). *Managing the madness: A practical guide to understanding young adolescents and classroom management.* Westerville, OH: Association for Middle Level Education.

Berckemeyer, J., & Kinney, P. (2005). *The what, why, and how of student-led conferences.* Westerville, OH: National Middle School Association.

Bergmann, S., & Brough, J. A. (2012). *Reducing the risk, increasing the promise.* Larchmont, NY: Eye on Education.

Bergmann, S., Brough, J.A., & Shepard, D. (2008). *Teach my kid I dare you: The educator's essential guide to parent involvement.* New York, NY: Routledge.

Brooks, R. (2013, 18 March). *2012 Dr. Robert Brooks definition of resiliency and the charismatic advisor.* [Video File]. Retrieved May 1, 2017, from https://www.youtube.com/watch?v=3P1rpDGiVNU

Brooks, R. (2015, April 14). *Resilience: The common underlying factor.* Retrieved May 1, 2017, from http://www.drrobertbrooks.com/resilience-common-underlying-factor/

Brooks, R., & Goldstein, S. (2002). *Raising resilient children: Fostering strength, hope, and optimism in your child.* New York, NY: McGraw-Hill.

Brooks, R., & Goldstein, S. (2004). *The power of resilience: Achieving balance, confidence, and personal strength in your life.* New York, NY: McGraw-Hill.

Carnegie Council on Adolescent Development. (1989). *Turning points: Preparing American youth for the 21st century.* Washington, DC: Carnegie Council on Adolescent Development.

Carnegie Council on Adolescent Development. (1995). *Great transitions: Preparing adolescents for a new century.* Washington, DC: Carnegie Council on Adolescent Development.

Center on the Developing Child at Harvard University. (2014). *Enhancing and practicing executive function skills with children from infancy to adolescence.* Retrieved May 1, 2017, from www.developingchild.harvard.edu

Center on the Developing Child at Harvard University. (2015). *Supportive relationships and active skill-building strengthen the foundations of resilience: Working paper No. 13.* Retrieved May 1, 2017, from http://developingchild.harvard.edu/resources/supportive-relationships-and-active-skill-building-strengthen-the-foundations-of-resilience/

Center on Education Policy. (2012). *Student motivation—An overlooked piece of school reform.* Retrieved May 1, 2017, from file:///Users/marjoriefrank/Downloads/UsherKober_Summary_Motivation_5.22.12.pdf

Centers for Disease Control and Prevention. (2009). *School connectedness: Strategies for increasing protective factors among youth.* Atlanta, GA: U.S. Department of Health and Human Services.

Clarkson, S., & Clarkson. S. (2016). *The lifegiving home: Creating a place of belonging and becoming.* Carol Stream, IL: Tyndale Momentum.

Clowes, G. (2011, Spring). The essential 5: A starting point for Kagan cooperative learning. *Kagan Online Magazine.* Retrieved May 1, 2017, from https://www.kaganonline.com/free_articles/research_and_rationale/330/The-Essential-5-A-Starting-Point-for-Kagan-Cooperative-Learning

Cohen, G. L., & Garcia, J. (2014). Educational theory, practice, and policy and the wisdom of social psychology. *Policy Insights from the Behavioral and Brain Sciences, 1*(1), 13-20.

Collaborative for Academic, Social, and Emotional Learning. (2017). *Core social and emotional learning competencies.* Retrieved May 1, 2017, from http://www.casel.org/core-competencies/

Comer, J. (1995). Lecture given at Education Service Center, Region IV. Houston, TX.

Cook-Sather, A. (2002). Authorizing students' perspectives: Toward trust, dialogue, and change in education. *Educational Researcher, 31*(4), 3-14.

Cook-Sather, A. (2006). Sound, presence, and power: "Student voice" in educational research and reform. *Curriculum Inquiry, 36*(4), 359-390.

Cornelius-White, J. (2007). Learner-centered teacher-student relationships are effective: A meta-analysis. *Review of Educational Research, 77,* 113-143.

Corwin & Quaglia School Voice. (2017). *Student voice Survey.* Retrieved May 1, 2017, from http://svsurveys.corwin.com/

Curwin, R. (2012, December 26). Believing in students: The power to make a difference. *Edutopia.* Retrieved May 1, 2017 from https://www.edutopia.org/blog/believing-in-students-richard-curwin

Cushman, K. (2009). *Fires in the middle school bathroom: Advice for teachers from middle schoolers.* New York, NY: The New Press.

Deci, E. L., with Flate, R. (1995). *Why we do what we do: Understanding self-motivation.* London, England: Gross/Putnam Books.

Deci, E.L., Koestner, R. & Ryan, R.M. (1999). A meta-analytic review of experiments examining the effects of extrinsic rewards on intrinsic motivation. *Psychological Bulletin, 125*(6), 627-668.

Deci, E. L., Koestner, R., & Ryan, R. M. (2001). Extrinsic rewards and intrinsic motivation in education: Reconsidered once again. *Review of Educational Research, 71*(1), 1-27.

Deci, E. L., & Ryan, R. M. (1985). *Intrinsic motivation and self-determination in human behavior.* New York, NY: Plenum Press.

Deci, E. L., & Ryan, R. M. (1987). The support of autonomy and the control of behavior. *Journal of Personality and Social Psychology, 53,* 1004-1037.

Dewey, J. (1913). *Interest and effort in education*. Ann Arbor, MI: University of Michigan Library.

Dweck, C. S. (2007). *Mindset: The new psychology of success*. New York, NY: Ballantine Books.

Dweck, C. S. (2010). Mindsets and equitable education. *Principal Leadership, 10*(5), 26-29.

Dweck, C. S. (2015). Carol Dweck revisits the "growth mindset." *Education Week Commentary, 35*(5), 20, 24.

Dweck, C. S., & Leggett, E. L. (1988). A social-cognitive approach to motivation and personality. *Psychological Review, 95*(2), 256.

Eichhorn, D. (1966) *The middle school*. New York, NY: Center for Applied Research in Education.

The Efficacy Institute. (2008). *Efficacy for students: Your tools for getting smart*. Retrieved May 1, 2017, from http://www.efficacy.org/Portals/7/Products/ Efficacy%20Secondary%20Workbook%20Demo.pdf

Ferguson, C. (2009). *Toolkit for Title I parent involvement*. Austin, TX: SEDL.

Fielding, M. (2001). Students as radical agents of change. *Journal of Educational Change, 2*(2), 123-141.

Fielding, M. (2004). Transformative approaches to student voice: Theoretical underpinnings, recalcitrant realities. *British Educational Research Journal, 30*(2), 343-354.

Fielding, M. (2006). Leadership, radical student engagement and the necessity of person-centered education. *International Journal of Leadership in Education, 9*(4), 299-313.

Fletcher, A. (2003a). Meaningful student involvement: A guide to inclusive school change. *SoundOut.org*. Retrieved May 1, 2017, from http://www.soundout.org/ MSIGuide.pdf

Fletcher, A. (2003b). *Unleashing student voice: Research supporting meaningful student involvement*. Olympia, WA: The Freechild Project.

Fletcher, A. (2013, January 23). *Teaching meaningful student involvement*. Retrieved May 1, 2017, from https://adamfletcher.net/ teaching-meaningful-student-involvement/

Fletcher, A. (2015, February 2). Why student voice? A research summary. *Soundout.org*. Retrieved May 1, 2017, from https://soundout.org/ why-student-voice-a-research-summary/

Flutter, J. (2007). Teacher development and pupil voice. *Curriculum Journal, 18*(3), 343-354.

Flutter, J., & Rudduck, J. (2004). *Consulting pupils: What's in it for schools?* London, England: Rougledge Falmer.

Fox, E. (2012). *Rainy brain, sunny brain: How to retrain your brain to overcome pessimism and achieve a more positive outlook*. New York, NY: Basic Books.

Fredricks, J. A., Blumenfeld, P. C., & Paris, A. H. (2004). School engagement: Potential of the concept, state of the evidence. *Review of Educational Research, 74*(1), 59-109.

Furrer, C., & Skinner, E. (2003). Sense of relatedness as a factor in children's academic engagement and performance. *Journal of Educational Psychology, 95*(1), 148-162.

Gonzalez, J. (2016, October 30). Is your lesson a Grecian urn? *Cult of Pedagogy.* Retrieved May 1, 2017, from http://www.cultofpedagogy.com/grecian-urn-lesson/

Goodenow, C. (1993). The psychological sense of school membership among adolescents: Scale development and educational correlates. *Psychology in the Schools, 30*(1), 70-90.

Gross-Loh, C. (2016, December 16). How praise became a consolation prize. *The Atlantic.* Retrieved May 1, 2017, from https://www.theatlantic.com/education/archive/2016/12/how-praise-became-a-consolation-prize/510845/

Guare, R., Dawson, P., & Guare, C. (2013). *Smart but scattered teens: The "Executive Skills" program for helping teens reach their potential.* New York, NY: The Guilford Press.

Guskey, T. R. (2011). Educational leadership: Effective grading practices. *Educational Leadership, 69*(3), 16-21.

Hazell, W. (2017, March 11). Malala tells heads they must help pupils believe in themselves. *TES School News International Magazine.* Retrieved May 1, 2017, from https://www.tes.com/news/school-news/breaking-news/malala-tells-heads-they-must-help-pupils-believe-themselves

Henderlong, J., & Lepper, M. (2002). The effects of praise on children's intrinsic motivation: A review and synthesis. *Psychological Bulletin, 128*, 774-795.

Henderson, A. T. & Mapp, K. L. (2002). *A new wave of evidence: The impact of school, family, and community connections on student achievement.* Washington, DC: Southwest Educational Development Laboratory.

Hoffman, A. & Field, S. (1995). Promoting self-determination through effective curriculum development. *Intervention in School and Clinic, 30*(3), 134-141.

Hoffman, J. (2017). Kids can cope: Parenting resilient children at home and at school. *Psychology Foundation of Canada.* Retrieved May 1, 2017, from http://cemh.lbpsb.qc.ca/parents/ResilienceChildrenBooklet.pdf

Iyengar, S. S., & Lepper, M. R. (2000). When choice is demotivating: Can one desire too much of a good thing? *Journal of Personality and Social Psychology, 79*(6), 995-1006.

Jensen, E. (2008). A fresh look at brain-based education. *Phi Delta Kappan Magazine 89*(6), 408-417.

Jetten, J., Haslam C., & Haslam, S. A. (2011). The case for a social identity analysis of health and well-being. In J. Jetten, C. Haslam, & S.A. Haslam (Eds.), *The social cure: Identity, health and well-being* (pp. 3-20). New York, NY: Psychology Press.

Kampakis, K. (2015). *10 truths middle schoolers should know.* Retrieved May 1, 2017, from http://www.karikampakis.com/2015/08/10-truths-middle-schoolers-should-know/.

Katz, I., & Assor, A. (2006, October). When choice motivates and when it does not. *Educational Psychology Review 19*(4): 429-442.

Kinney, P. (2012). *Fostering student accountability through student-led conferences.* Westerville, OH: Association for Middle Level Education.

Kohlberg, L. (1963). The development of children's orientations toward a moral order: I. Sequence in the development of moral thought. *Vita Humana, 6*(1-2), 11–33.

Kohn, A. (1993). *Punished by rewards: The trouble with gold stars, incentive plans, A's, praise, and other bribes.* Boston, MA: Houghton Mifflin.

Kohn, A. (2001). Five reasons to stop saying, "Good job!" *Young Children 56*(5), 24-28.

Komives, S. R., Dugan, J. P., Owen, J. E., Slack, C., & Wagner, W. (Eds.) (2011). *The handbook for student leadership development (2nd ed.).* San Francisco, CA: JosseyBass.

Krakovsky, M. (2007, March/April). The effort effect. *Stanford Alumni Magazine.* Retrieved May 1, 2017, from https://alumni.stanford.edu/get/page/magazine/article/?article_id=32124

Lepper, M., Greene, D., & Nisbett, R. E. (1973). Undermining children's intrinsic interests with extrinsic reward. *Journal of Personality and Social Psychology, 28*(1), 129-137.

Levin, B. (2000). Putting students at the centre of education reform. *Journal of Educational Change, 1*(2), 155-172.

Levine, M. (2012, August 4). Raising successful children. *The New York Times Sunday Review.* Retrieved May 1, 2017, from http://www.nytimes.com/2012/08/05/opinion/sunday/raising-successful-children.html

Lewis, J., Hunter, M., & Green, A. (2009, February). Teaching student leadership in an inner-city school. *AMLE Magazine.* Retrieved May 1, 2017, from https://www.amle.org/BrowsebyTopic/WhatsNew/WNDet/TabId/270/ArtMID/888/ArticleID/136/Teaching-Student-Leadership-in-an-Inner-City-School.aspx

Libbey, H. P. (2004). Measuring student relationships to school: Attachment, bonding, connectedness, and engagement. *Journal of School Health, 74*(7), 275-283.

Libbey, H. P. (2007). *School connectedness: Influence above and beyond family connectedness.* Ann Arbor, MI: University of Michigan ProQuest Information and Learning Company.

Litchfield Historical Society. (1968). *My Country, 2*(3), 23.

Lounsbury, J. H. (2000). Understanding and appreciating the wonder years. Retrieved May 1, 2017, from https://www.amle.org/portals/0/pdf/mlem/wonder_years.pdf

MacBeath, J., Demetriou, H., Rudduck, J., & Myers K. (2003). *Consulting pupils: A toolkit for teachers.* Cambridge: Pearson Publishing.

Martin, A.J., & Dowson, M. (2009). Interpersonal relationships, motivation, engagement, and achievement: Yields for theory, current issues, and educational practice. *Review of Educational Research, 79,* 327-365.

Matthews, M. (2015). Student leadership development: A literature review and focus group interview on leadership education. *University of Wyoming Doctoral Projects, Masters Plan B, and Related Works. Paper 8.* Retrieved May 1, 2017, from http://repository.uwyo.edu/cgi/viewcontent.cgi?article=1007&context=plan

McCombs, B. L., & Whisler, J. S. (1997). *The learner-centered classroom and school: Strategies for increasing student motivation and achievement.* San Francisco, CA: Jossey-Bass.

McIntyre, D., Pedder, D., & Ruddick, J. (2005). Pupil voice: Comfortable and uncomfortable learnings for teachers. *Research Papers in Education, 20*(2), 149-168. Cambridge, UK: University of Cambridge.

Mitra, D. (2004). The significance of students: Can increasing student voice in schools lead to gains in youth development? *The Teachers College Record, 106*(4), 651-688.

Morehead, J. (2012, June 19). Stanford University's Carol Dweck on the growth mindset and education. *OneDublin.org.* Retrieved May 1, 2017, from https://onedublin.org/2012/06/19/stanford-universitys-carol-dweck-on-the-growth-mindset-and-education/

Mozhgan, A., Parivash, J., Nadergholi, G., & Jowkar, B. (2011). Student leadership competencies development. *Procedia Social and Behavioral Sciences, 15*, 1616-1620.

National Association of Secondary School Principals. (2006). *Breaking ranks in the middle: Strategies for leading middle level reform.* Reston, VA: Author.

National Middle School Association [NMSA]. (2010). *This we believe: Keys to educating young adolescents.* Westerville, OH: Author.

O'Brien, K. A., & Bowles, T. (2013). The importance of belonging for adolescents in secondary school settings. *The European Journal of Social & Behavioural Sciences, ISSN:2301-2218,* 1-9.

Osterman, K. F. (2000). Students' need for belonging in the school community. *Review of Educational Research, 70*(3), 323-367.

Patall, E. A., Cooper, H., & Robinson, J. C. (2008). The effects of choice on intrinsic motivation and related outcomes: A meta-analysis of research findings. *Psychological Bulletin, 134*(2), 270–300.

Patall, E. A., Cooper, H., & Wynn, S. R. (2010). The effectiveness and relative importance of choice in the classroom. *Journal of Educational Psychology (102)*4, 896-915.

Pedder, D. (2009). Student voice: Cultivating conversations, reaching the unconsulted majority. *Learning & Teaching Update 25.*

Pedder, D., McIntyre, D. (2006). Pupil consultation: The importance of social capital. *Educational Review, 58*(2), 145-157.

Pink, D. (2011). *Drive: The surprising truth about what motivates us.* New York, NY: Penguin Group.

Pounds, J. (2014, May 17). Class teaches leadership skills to middle school students. *The News & Adventure.* Retrieved May 1, 2017, from http://www.newsadvance.com/news/local/class-teaches-leadership-skills-to-middle-school-students/article_1d22d924-dd78-11e3-ba28-0017a43b2370.html

Quaglia Institute. (2017). *Our Framework: 8 Conditions*. Retrieved from http://qisa.org/framework/conditions.jsp

Rattan, A., Good, C., & Dweck, C. S. (2012). "It's ok—not everyone can be good at math": Instructors with an entity theory comfort (and demotivate) students. *Journal of Experimental Social Psychology, 48*(3), 731-737.

Reeve, J., Jang, H., Carrell, D., Jeon, S., & Barch, J. (2004). Enhancing students' engagement by increasing teachers' autonomy support. *Motivation and Emotion, 28*, 147.

Reeve, J., Nix, G., & Hamm, D. (2003). Testing models of experience of self determination in intrinsic motivation and the conundrum of choice. *Journal of Educational Psychology, 95*, 375-392.

Rimm-Kaufman, S., & Sandilos, L. (2011). Improving students' relationships with teachers to provide essential supports for learning. *American Psychological Association*. Retrieved May 1, 2017, from http://www.apa.org/education/k12/relationships.aspx

Romero, C. (2015). What we know about belonging from scientific research. *Mindset Scholars Network*. Retrieved May 1, 2017, from mindsetscholarsnetwork.org/wp-content/.../What-We-Know-About-Belonging.pdf

Rosch, D., & Meixner, C. (2011). Powerful pedagogies. In S. R. Komives, J.P. Dugan, J. E. Owen, C. Slack, & W. Wagner (Eds.), *The handbook for student leadership development* (pp. 307-337). San Francisco, CA: Jossey-Bass.

Rosenthal, R., & Jacobson, L. (1968). *Pygmalion in the classroom*. The Urban Review, 3(1), 16-20.

Rudduck, J., & McIntyre, D. (2007). *Improving learning through consulting pupils*. London, England: Routledge.

Ryan, R. M., & Deci, E. L. (2000a). Intrinsic and extrinsic motivation: Classic definitions and new directions. *Contemporary Educational Psychology, 25*(1), 54-67.

Ryan, R. M., & Deci, E. L. (2000b). Self-determination theory and the facilitation of intrinsic motivation, social development, and well-being. *American Psychologist, 55*(1), 68-78.

Ryan, R. M., & Deci, E. L. (2017). *Self-determination theory: Basic psychological needs in motivation, development, and wellness*. New York, NY: The Guilford Press.

Schaps, E. (2003). Creating a school community. *Educational Leadership, 60*(6), 31-33.

Schaps, E., Battistich, V., & Solomon. (2003). Community in school as key to student growth: Findings from the Child Development Project. *Caring communities and education, Chapter 9*. Oakland, CA: Developmental Studies Center.

Scherer, M. (September 2006). Celebrate strengths, nurture affinities: A conversation with Mel Levine. *Educational Leadership 64*(1), 8-15.

Seligman, M. E. (2006). *Learned optimism: How to change your mind and your life*. New York, NY: Vintage.

Sharot, T. (2011). *The optimism bias: A tour of the irrationally positive brain*. New York, NY: Pantheon.

Silver, D. (2012). *Fall down 7 times, get up 8: Teaching kids to succeed.* Thousand Oaks, CA: Corwin and Westerville, OH: Association for Middle Level Education.

Silver, D., Berckemeyer, J., & Baenen, J. (2015). *Deliberate optimism: Reclaiming the joy in education.* Thousand Oaks, CA: Corwin.

Silver, D., & Stafford, D. (2017). *Teaching kids to thrive: Essential skills for success.* Thousand Oaks, CA: Corwin.

Stepp, L. S. (2001). *Our last best shot: Guiding our children through early adolescence.* New York, NY: Berkley Publishing Group.

Sternberg, R. J. (2000). Wisdom as a form of giftedness. *Gifted Child Quarterly, 44*(4), 252-259.

Sternberg, R. J., & Grigorenko, E. L. (2000). *Teaching for successful intelligence.* Arlington Heights, IL: Skylight Training.

Swaim, S., & Kinney, P. (2009). *Voices of experience: Perspectives from successful middle level leaders.* Westerville, OH: National Middle School Association and National Association of Secondary School Principals.

United Nations General Assembly. (1989). *Convention on the rights of the child.* General Assembly Resolution A 44/25. Retrieved May 1, 2017, from http://www.un.org/documents/ga/res/44/a44r025.htm

Van Velsor, E., & Wright, J. (2012). *Expanding the leadership equation: Developing next-generation leader.* ERIC: Center for Creative Leadership White Paper. Retrieved May 1, 2017, from http://files.eric.ed.gov/fulltext/ED543117.pdf

Whitaker, T. (2013). *What great teachers do differently: 17 things that matter most.* New York, NY: Routledge.

Wilcox, K. C. (with Angelis, J. I.). (2007). *What makes middle schools work.* Albany, NY: University at Albany School of Education Albany Institute for Research in Education.

Williamson, R. (2009, March). The schedule as a tool to improve student learning. *Instructional Leader, 22*(3), 1-4.

Wingspread. (2004). Wingspread declaration on school connections. *Journal of School Health, 74,* 233-234.

Wormeli, R. [Stenhouse Publishers]. (2010, 14 December). *Rick Wormeli: Redos, retakes, and do-overs, part one.* [Video File]. Retrieved May 1, 2017, from https://www.youtube.com/watch?v=TM-3PFfIfvI

Wormeli, R. (2011). Redos and retakes done right. *Educational Leadership, 69*(3), 22-26.

Wormeli, R. (2013, August). Looking at executive function, *AMLE Magazine.* Retrieved May 1, 2017, from https://www.amle.org/BrowsebyTopic/WhatsNew/WNDet/TabId/270/ArtMID/888/ArticleID/298/Looking-at-Executive-Function.aspx

Wormeli, R. (2016, 25 September). The right way to do redos. *Middleweb.* Retrieved May 1, 2017, from https://www.middleweb.com/31398/rick-wormeli-the-right-way-to-do-redos/

About the Authors

Laurie Barron

Currently in her twenty-second year in education, Laurie is superintendent of the Evergreen School District, Kalispell, Montana. She previously served as a high school English teacher and coach, a middle school assistant principal, a middle school principal in Newnan, Georgia, and she has served as a part-time assistant professor at the university level. Laurie is a board member for the Association for Middle Level Education and was named as one of the University of Georgia Alumni Association's "40 Under 40" recipients.

Laurie is a National Board Certified Teacher and was honored as a Teacher of the Year and STAR Teacher. Her work as the principal of Smokey Road Middle School in Newnan, Georgia, led to her selection as the 2012 Georgia Middle School Principal of the Year, 2013 MetLife/NASSP National Middle Level Principal of the Year, and Smokey Road Middle School's selection as a one of five middle schools in the nation to be named a 2011 MetLife Foundation-NASSP Breakthrough School.

Laurie holds a BSEd in English Education from the University of Georgia, an MEd in Supervision and Administration from the University of West Georgia, and an EdS and EdD in Educational Leadership from the University of Sarasota. She also studied at Oxford University in England. Laurie co-authored the book *What Parents Need to Know about Common Core and Other College- and Career-Ready Standards.*

Patti Kinney

Patti has been an elementary school teacher, a middle school teacher when her district made the transition to middle school in the mid-80s, and has been involved in staff development as well as teaching at Southern Oregon University. As an assistant principal and later principal of Talent Middle School, she was highly involved in the process to transform this former 7-8 junior high school into a 6-8 middle school, which later was recognized as one of "100 highly successful middle schools" in a national research study sponsored by the National Association of Secondary School Principals (NASSP).

Patti is a past president of the Association for Middle Level Education and of the Oregon Middle Level Association. In 2007, she was awarded the Oregon Middle Level Association's first Distinguished Service Award that was also named in her honor. She was named the Oregon Assistant Principal of the Year in 1996, the Oregon Principal of the Year in 2002, and in 2003, was selected as the MetLife/NASSP National Middle Level Principal of the Year. From 2007 through 2014, she served as associate director, middle level services for NASSP.

Patti currently speaks, presents, and consults on middle level issues at the national and international levels. She has authored the book *Fostering Student Accountability through Student-led Conferences* and co-authored three books: *Voices of Experience: Perspectives from Middle Level Leaders; What Parents Need to Know about Common Core and Other College- and Career-Ready Standards;* and *The What, Why, and How of Student-Led Conferences.*